LIVING WITH DIRTY GLASSES

LEAH SPELT LIGIA

Defining Moments Press, Inc.

Copyright © Leah Montani, 2021

Disclaimer

Cover Design: 99 Designs

Editing: Joy Montgomery

Contents

To learn more and connect with Leah here:

Download your PDF workbook to start cleaning your dirty glasses:

SCAN HERE

Or visit: www.leahspeltligia.com

Follow on these platforms below

Or email leahspeltligia@gmail.com

Dedication

To Bob for always seeing in me what I couldn't and holding the dream while I grew into it. Thank you. Thank you for being the glue to help piece me back together and believe in a bigger dream.

To my children, thank you for your love and patience and teaching me to be the mom you need, for being my reason and inspiration to continue to strive and grow to pass down all I've learned.

To Esther, my dearest friend for always holding space and the best of hugs, showing up and knowing what to say and keep me on track.

To my mom for your strength and courage in the face of adversity. It's been the greatest joy of my life to watch you come alive.

To all those have helped me on the journey, held my hand, cleaned up my mess, welcomed me in as a stray, held space for my tears, saw the best in me when I couldn't see anything in front of me, my deepest and sincerest thanks.

All the pieces I've picked up along the journey have made me who I am.

To the reader on the path, may you find the courage to clean your dirty glasses and experience a new way of seeing your world.

Scars

My scars are not worn
outside for all to see
they are hidden inside of me.

I hide them with smiles,
addictions, and
all the things I can do.

I try to ignore them,
but they wail and
stick to me like glue.

The pain I try to drown out,
memories I can't stop
myself from seeing.

Relentless chatter,
critical drivers,
all cranking up anxiety.

We all have scars
we wear inside.
ones we hide,
ones still healing,
ones still bleeding.

Let go... to start the healing....

(Leah's journal 2002)

Introduction

Did you ever wake up and think to yourself, "Come on why can't you just let this go?" You go through life feeling like you can handle things, life is going pretty well then...

BOOM!

It feels like it's all crashing down; your insides are a jumbled emotional mess.

One minute everything is making you angry. The next, a small act of kindness is bringing you to tears. In another, you are experiencing jabs of jealously; you're agitated and have a short fuse. You don't want to get up in the morning. Everything feels so damn hard.

You think, "Where is this coming from?"

You start feeling self-conscious and try to hide the hard emotions. You try to put on your happy smile. All the while, your insides are churning and it feels like a raging storm is flooding you from within. "Just get through the day. Just keep going. Just get through the day. Tomorrow will be better." You try to convince yourself but it starts all over again... until you have that good day again.

This was the rollercoaster I was living. I didn't become fully aware of this until I was pregnant with my second child. Hormones and fatigue exaggerated the drops into depression, I'd have panic attacks that felt like they came out of nowhere.

I'd be in line at a store and see the scenes of my life flash through my head leaving me breathless and distressed. What was going on? There were days I felt so down I could barely come to the surface for air.

I moved around my world cautiously, never knowing when it would happen. I went about my days just trying to get through the next wave of intense emotion. Other days, I acted out badly, I'd be defensive, reactive, always on guard.

During that season, I'd feel the cold grip of shame and guilt wrap itself around me. Shame for not being better, shame for being so damn pitiful, guilt that I kept making the same mistakes. It felt like, no matter how hard I tried, I just couldn't get it right. I took refuge in staying as busy as possible. That seemed to keep my demons at bay.

I filled up every spare moment of my time and as much as I ran from it, tried to hide it, tried to ignore it, I'd find myself in a tearful heap on the phone desperate to call someone but feeling too ashamed and guilty to bring myself to actually do it.

I am a grown adult. No one has time for this bullshit.

I was the person who was fun and lively, full of energy and life, I was responsible for caring for children of my own and in my community. What would they think of me? What would they say? They might think I am not up for the task.

Instead, I just stayed silent and did the very best thing I thought I could do.

I did more.

I am capable of this job. I am an excellent caregiver. I poured myself more into my work and family. Baking and making food from scratch, creating an Early Childhood Education curriculum, going to school part-time, volunteering at the women's shelter, taking Karate. Go! Go! Go!

Anything to prove to myself and my little family that I was worthy of their love. Anything to prove to my clients who trusted me with their children that I was worthy of their trust.

In the few quiet moments, I had to myself, my tears would overflow in the shower.

What is wrong with me?

I could never do enough; I was never enough. I hated myself when I was by myself. When people came with complements, I could only hear the voice inside say, "If you only knew who I really was."

I look back on that version of myself and I feel great compassion for her. I want to take her in my arms and give her the strongest, most loving hug and tell her. I want to tell her that she is stronger than she knows; she is brave and beautiful and she will change the world.

She just doesn't know it yet.

I wish I could go back and tell her to trust in her intuition, stand up for herself, listen to the whispering of her heart. "No, darling, you don't have to do that. You don't have to let them walk all over you. You don't have to keep quiet. You don't have to do it all."

They see the very best parts of you, why can't you?

For years I found myself drawn to personal development books but I was so self-conscious about reading them that I stopped, not knowing the gift and time I had discarded.

I was on a reckless path to burnout and self-sabotage, desperate to get away from the self I had been in my teens.

The self that was hospitalized for almost two years to protect me from... myself.

As if feeling so desperate that I wanted to end my life wasn't enough, I came to realize that, among the great many things I was terrible at in my life, I couldn't even get this one thing right.

Thank goodness! With success, I wouldn't be able to tell you all the things I have learned on my journey. It wasn't until I saw the brink of death that I came to see all life's beauty.

I had given up on trying to make sense of my world, the violence, the manipulation, the alienation, the abandonment, the home that fell apart, the constant state of fear I was in.

I didn't have a guide to help me understand what I was going through. I didn't have the manual to explain these intense feelings I was having, or why I was having them, much less what to do about it. I didn't have the safety of home.

This is why I have dedicated the past 18 years to reading personal development books, working with life coaches, attending workshops, seminars, audio books, writing, journaling and looking for any resource I could to understand what was happening inside me. What did it mean? It has allowed me to shift my life and rewrite the narrative that was keeping me small, hidden and scared, stuck in the loop of pain and shame. I couldn't live on that roller coaster any more. It was robbing the most precious of gifts, life.

When you feel out of control, this lingering dread affects every aspect of your life, how you relate and interact with others, how you show up and contribute, or don't.

It looks like hiding and making excuses. It looks anti-social and always avoiding interactions. It looks like drinking a little too much to stay numb. It looks like life moving at a snail's pace while you are in the grips of pain but then looking up when you get through and seeing that days or months have passed and you are still suffering, a little older, a little wiser and even more in despair.

There is a way out.

A note of Caution:

My dear reader – I must tell you, as you go down this path, about some tools that will help you through: a fresh journal, pens that feel joyful in your hands, your most favourite cup of comfort, (mine is coffee with just a splash of milk. Yours might be tea or cocoa.) and most importantly an open mind.

Remember you are brave, strong and capable. I challenge you to stay open, though your discomfort will demand otherwise. You've lived closed off this far and, as a consequence, have closed off a piece of yourself.

A recent experience to illustrate:

This very book you are reading has been in my heart for over 5 years, maybe even longer. I have started and stopped so many times but this time was different.

This time, I surrounded myself with other authors, and people on a mission who would hold me accountable, people who had done the very thing I was trying and failing to do for 5 years. In the process, it came to the point where I actually had to write the book on a deadline. As I went through the process of understanding my why, I shared with the group and a mentor, my story and vision.

Through this group and mentorship, I created a vision for the life I wanted that made me feel vibrant, alive and excited. I discovered a passion for public speaking and storytelling and wanted to share the lessons and hope I had learned along the way.

I had created this vision again and again in my mind's eye. I was committed, enthusiastic, I invested time, money and countless efforts into this dream. As I approached the deadline for this book, I was surprised to find the end goal was suddenly feeling unreachable.

I could feel old companions resurface, Doubt and Fear whispering in my ear, "This is unrealistic and childish". Despite all my years of learning and training I felt helpless to stop the flood of negativity descending upon me. "You are a phony. Who do you think you are? How are YOU going to do that? You have no experience. You can't even come up with a real business. You are a financial mess. You can't get anything right. You call that a chapter? It hardly makes sense.
No one is going to read this. It's trash. You're trash." On and on the taunts went – my inner bullies out for some fun.

I've done enough meditation, self-awareness exercises, and journaling to see what was happening but I didn't know how to stop the oppressors. I was coming face-to-face with the one thing I have been resisting the most, the one thing that makes me vulnerable, that exposes my most tender side.

I kept with my habits and I started my workout. Keep moving forward. I turned on my headphones and, then, in the middle of the work out, a thought rocked me to my core.

When we are not being who we truly 'know' we are, there is a part inside us that is dying to be heard, to be seen. It's the part of us that is true and real, the part we keep hidden and far from the light, to protect us, keep us safe. Who I am is always changing because I am always changing? I am. I am...

In that moment it all made sense. There, in my unfinished basement, I took a piece of chalk and wrote down 2 words, 2 column headings.

WAS to the left of me, AM to the right.

I started writing down all the aspects of who I was.

I share this with you because I wish I had known that healing and growth is not a switch. It is a process - one that will bring new insights and understanding to your experience as you move forward.

Even though it has been over 18 years of work, I still make huge leaps. Still learn new things. Still, forever, the student. Each insight is another step on my path.

I wrote, under "WAS": Broken, victim, helpless, anxious, depressed, broke, abandoned, unloved, flawed, discarded, alone, scared.

Then, under "AM" I wrote: strong, leader, powerful, creator, student, teacher, joyful, abundant, vibrant, focused, driven, bold, courageous, brave, loved.

As I looked at my chalk chart, I saw what was happening. I had been struggling for the past two days, trying to talk about it, write it, meditate on it, ignore it. Then, there it was!

I am a person who sees the world in pictures and when I saw those lists on the floor, I saw the desperate me trying to claw me back so I would not leave her behind.

The me that has been there, my fear, and my insecurities, had been my closest companions and my heaviest chains. They were trying so hard to keep me with them, preventing me from believing that I was above them, I was past this. Refusing to accept I didn't need them anymore.

They lay dormant as I kept moving, paying little attention. I had gotten past them but now I faced the very thing I had been avoiding for years, the thing that makes me feel exposed and self-conscious. I faced the very thing I felt my heart kept calling me to do.

Confronting that fear awoke my insecurities and uncertainties with a ferocity and strength I hadn't known in a long time.

Your fears live in darkness. Your shame cannot survive the light. Pain lives in silence. I did this crazy thing. I thanked them. I thanked all the past versions of me.

I thanked them for being there for me, for protecting me and keeping me as safe as they could. I couldn't listen to them anymore but, if they wanted to still be a part of my life, they were welcome to sit in the back seat. They were not allowed to drive anymore.

If this sounds fantastical, let me ask you, "Are your negative thoughts any different?" The absurdities you tell yourself, how have they served you?

In acknowledging my past selves and thanking them for their service, the grip of inaction dissipated. The panic I was feeling evaporated. I felt free again.

I tell you this story to impress upon you that our minds are powerful and seductive. It takes commitment and consistency to grow out of your pain and into forgiveness for yourself.

If you'd like to try this, pull out a piece of paper, an empty cement floor, a wall, a canvas, your arm, and write WAS on one side and AM on the other. Write down all the WAS characteristics you had, even if it is something you are struggling with still to this day.

Now, on the other side, I want you to get your dreaming glasses on and imagine the brightest most beautiful (AM) version of you. I don't care if it feels unrealistic to you right now. What does this person do? How do they interact with others? What is important to them? How do they contribute? You don't have to be there yet but it's important to set that picture in your mind of the person you want to be, even if you aren't convinced it's possible… yet. We will get to that.

As you go through this book, I weave together stories of the past to help illustrate the foundations that got me to that desperate state I was in with stories that helped me find my way out and be the person I am today. I've littered the book with quotes that anchor me during particularly turbulent storms, quotes that remind me it is time to grow, that help me make sense of my experience and remind me I am not alone, and make me ask "What is the story behind the person who said it?"

Most of all I want you to know you are not alone. The thoughts, the feelings, the experiences are all part of the ingredients that make you uniquely you.

Though our experience and pain may not be the same, we are here together because we want something more than this baggage.

There is so much more. I pray you find hope and light in the pages ahead and find the courage to clean your glasses.

All my love and light;

Leah, Spelt Ligia

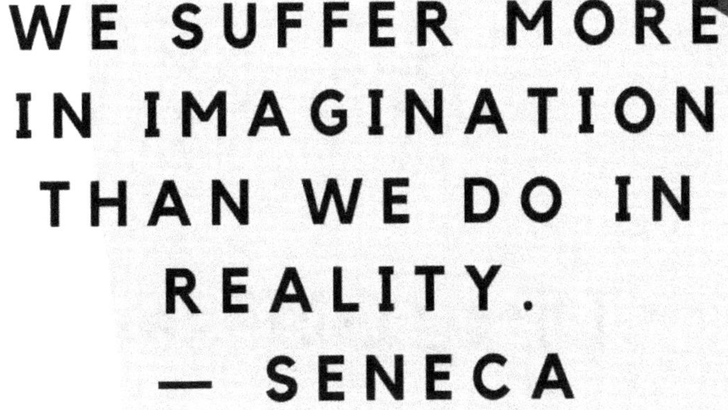
WE SUFFER MORE
IN IMAGINATION
THAN WE DO IN
REALITY.
— SENECA

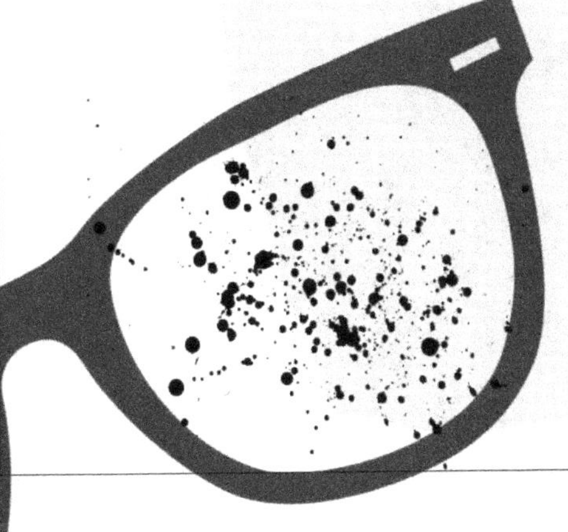

Part 1:

Dirty Glasses

Chapter 1 – Dirty Glasses: Finding Peace with Your Past

I've worn glasses for as long as I can remember. I remember the day my curiosity got the best of me. I was 3 years old. It's one of my earliest memories - one I share later on in the book. Since then, I've worn glasses and, for many of those years, my dad cleaned my glasses. As a glasses wearer himself, he recognized the need and value in the habit.

When the responsibility was shifted to me, however, I was not as devoted to the task. I have never been really great at being consistent with proper eyewear care. It's usually not until I catch a reflection of a splatter in the mirror, or wonder why my eyes are burning, or feel a headache coming on that I think, "Hey! Maybe I should clean my glasses."

There are times that I go to put them on and I see they could use a quick wash but think, "Nah, they are still good I can see just fine."

What do dirty glasses have to do with empathy?

The term, "looking through rose-colored glasses" comes to mind. The idea that when we are in awe or deep appreciation of what we are looking at, we have rose colored glasses; we want to see things even better than they are. Typically, this happens in a new love, a long sought-after car, or a new job.

We only see what is amazing and great about it, wondering how we could have gone this long without it. We look past annoying habits, defects and limitations, convincing ourselves that it's perfect as it is. We become accustomed to this level of expectation. As humans, our natural instinct is to want for something even better. Eventually, the rose color wears off and things that didn't enter our awareness are, suddenly, a source of agitation and frustration.

If this is the effect of rose-colored glasses, what is the result of glasses left dirty, scratched, maybe even with the wrong prescription?

Glasses left uncleaned and marred with the evidence of our daily living affect how we perceive the stories of our lives. Leaving us with unclear views, narrow focus and distorted images of our LIVING WITH DIRTY GLASSES environment. Our eyes strain to try and correct the image and fill in the gaps.

Our, poor over worked eyes respond with the physical signs of fatigue, drying out and sore, watering excessively trying to compensate, further blurring our vision causing headaches, increased sensitivity to light and difficulty concentrating. Believe it or not, eyes that need to work so hard to achieve clear focus can cause tension in our necks, and shoulders, compensating in response.

All this from ignoring dirty glasses!

This is the effect of carrying our dirty glasses from our painful past. As an adult who could "do it better", we view our past through the lens of a child trying to get by, with the grief of a life you will never have.

As we emerge into adulthood, we might still carry our childhood perceptions that we haven't quite figured out how to grow out of. We often don't realize that we were supposed to grow out of them.

What if we took off those glasses and tried a new prescription, one more fit for our adult-eyes - one that is clean and clear allowing us to see the whole picture?

What would that life look like?

Would you find peace? Would you understand things differently? Would you have the space you need to forgive and let the past stay where it is?

This is my journey through my process of changing my dirty glasses for a better fitting pair - one that empowers me. It has allowed me to acknowledge and process traumas and hurts I didn't even realize I was carrying that have held me back from being the person I want to be. All these things I wish I could go back 20 years and tell my hurting self.

The hope, in sharing this story, is that you take the gifts of hope, an idea or maybe a habit to help you on your journey to calm the hurt, to realize your strength and to remember why it matters, to realize why you matter, to realize why this one precious life matters to you, to learn to give grace to the most undeserving of that kindness.

Someone asked me "Why do you want to do this?" Tears streamed and an unexpected answer came in the next breath, "I don't want anyone to feel as alone as I once did."

You are not alone in your pain. You don't have to stay trapped there either.

It's time to clean our glasses and find healing by shifting our perceptions, challenging our stories, giving ourselves empathy for doing the best we could with the limited resources and sense of awareness we had.

How much longer are you going to carry the weight of knowing, deep down, you were made for so much more? How much longer are you going to live the watered-down version of you?

Let's get to work cleaning those glasses. Imagine the clarity and peace when you have glasses meant for you. It's up to you to keep them clean. Life will throw dirt at you every now and then, and the trick is keeping them clean over time before they cause those painful headaches.

"ONE CAN CHOOSE TO GO BACK TOWARD SAFETY OR FORWARD TOWARD GROWTH.

GROWTH MUST BE CHOSEN AGAIN AND AGAIN; FEAR MUST BE OVERCOME AGAIN AND AGAIN."

-ABRAHAM MASLOW

Chapter 2 – Contrast: Life Is a Mystery

The evening is whispering its way in through the windows surrounded by coffee-colored bricks fumbling to stay together around the worn edges of the window frame. Slight drafts creep in unnoticed, almost welcomed in the warmth of a bright fall day. The hues of scarlet, gold, and pumpkin orange flicker in the light drawing stained glass images along the floor.

"Please, Daddy? Please? Just one song. I have to show you. Pllllleeeeeaaassse? just one song. I have a new dance! Pleeasse?" Her eyes were wide and pleading, promising to give him her very best.

He looks down into those soft hazel brown eyes. Flecks of gold scatter across them with veins of emerald that remind him of his mother. Her hair is tousled and sticking to her face, a mix of sweat and heat. She is flush with excitement and energy.

"I promise I'll go to bed after. I promise I'm going to brush my teeth and everything. I won't just run my toothbrush under the sink I'll put the spicy goop in my mouth and I will scrub. I promise! Please? It's only like 5 minutes. I've been practicing alllll day. PLEEASSE, DADDY, PLLLLEEEEEEAAAAASE?"

At 4 and a bit, Ligia Elena (your author), or better known as Gigi to him, has long dark chocolate-colored hair that falls past her shoulders, wild with the adventures of the day, pieces of grass and leaves littered throughout it. She has her mini white handheld cassette player firmly in hand, her favorite artist, cued and ready.

She has been rehearsing for her audience of forest friends and her nearest and dearest friend, Puffy-Puff, a not so snow-white puffball Popple she takes with her everywhere. She has been waiting for THIS. Every spare moment she is dancing and rocking out to her favorite singer, pop legend, and sensation: Madonna.

The faint smell of pork, smothered with achote (a Spanish seasoning that brings with it the familiarity of Nicaragua, of home, family, scorching heat and humidity, open spaces littered with huge plants, stretching and reaching to touch the rays of the sun), and steamed vegetables, still fills the room.

The hum of running water, clanking dishes and pans from the kitchen provide the background to her pleas as Mama cleans up the dinner plates. Papa is in charge of putting pepita (little girl) to bed.

The room is getting darker with light fading from the window and slowly being eaten up by the toffee brown curtains. Parquet flooring is smooth and scuffed by time and feet.

"Paaaapa Please. My heart begs you. I neeeeed to show you."

"Ok Pepita. Dale pues." (Ok, my sweetheart, go on, let's do the show).

How can he say no? She's been practicing ALLL day.

Her whole being lights up. She flings herself into his arms and hugs him so tight that Papa's dinner is shuffled around and he burps.

She erupts in giggles

"PAPA!" She scolds.

"Excuse me! Excuse me! I couldn't help it! It was you!" he says.

She stumbles over herself to set up and get into position. Her cassette is set. She runs and grabs her shimmering black-sequined hat and scarf in her bedroom. She can't forget her secret weapon - a pair of red patent dress shoes from Abuelita (her grandma).

"Just one song", he reminds her with his head tilted and looking at her for confirmation of their deal.

"Then straight to bed."

She looks at him. Eyes lock, "I Promise" she vows.

The room is dark now except for the light of a table lamp. That's all she needs. She stands still, in position.

Waiting. Listening. Organ's chime. The soft pleading voice of Madonna fills the air.

"Life is a mystery.

Everyone must stand alone.

I hear you call my name and it feels like home."

Drums pick up in the background, the cowbell clanks, Ligia bursts to life, shaking and jumping to the rhythm letting it move and guide her little body. As Madonna sets into prayer, her movements slow and she drops to her knees looking for answers in the sky.

As graceful as a well-rounded 4-year-old with limbs she's still growing into can gather, she lifts and pirouettes. Crouching and folding as the youth of her muscles flex and bend.

She feels the music. She is lifted by the beat.

"I close my eyes. OH God I think I am falling…. Heaven help me…."

She hops and bops walking away and reaching back holding her hand out. Like a dream, she wants to bring you into her world. She's inviting you to come to see where she lives.

As the music starts to slow before the finale, she is so in sync. The song ramps up and she fidgets and bops across the floor into a slide then tosses her hat to the audience and walks off the stage as the music fades.

She runs back and slides down on her knees air mike in hand, Madonna sings and she mouths the words with her idol.

The enthusiasm and performance were so infectious and filled the room with pride and joy only a father can know. Seeing his little girl perform with such energy and spirit.

After the initial song (and 3 songs that followed after that), Papa finally said it was time to go to bed. He applauded her.

"Bravo, Gigi! Bravo! You are quite the dancer."

She ran into him, all sweaty and breathless.

"Thank you! I love to dance." She stopped her mini boom box and ran off to her room.

"Uh uh! Teeth, Gigi".

"Oh, Papa I was going, I'm just putting my radio away".

It wasn't long after that she was enrolled in dance classes. A Minnie Mouse ballet class. These classes were fun but were too limited for her enthusiasm, though she did get a chance to perform on stage.

Just over a decade later – "How did I get here?" I ask myself as icy, February winds sting my tear-stained face. My cheeks are burning and the color of poinsettias in December. I wait there, just outside the car. Fumes rising, I cough and wrap my arms around myself. Not so much from the cold but to brace myself for what's coming next.

My dad, who just drove me into town an hour away from home, tosses out the duffle bag I packed haphazardly in the 5 minutes he gave me to pack before he threw me out the front door. Only to open the door back up and demand I get back inside. Frozen in shock and still hurting from the tussle I didn't move. Impatient he came out and hauled me back in the house shoving a phone in my face. "Call, figure out where ever you need to go. Here you will not stay."

I scrambled to figure out who to call. I called my psychiatrist but the line was busy.

In the living room I can see mom's back slumped over a chair. I don't see her face but I hear her crying. I hear dad talking to her about the poison in the family. "She's nothing but a cancer." I hear snippets. "There is nothing more for us to do. She…"

Beep, beep, beep the busy signal rings.

Who could I call? My friends were in school. My mom's family? I wouldn't dare. I don't even know how to reach them. I could hear him coming back.

"Time's up. Let's go."

The ride into town was silent, giving me time to reflect on what had happened.

Was he throwing me out? Was it about the smoke mom caught me having in the shower? No. Was it because I snuck out to a friend's house for a few hours?

Mom had grounded me already for the smoking. I didn't do it again.

Here we go again. It didn't matter where we were, the move, the new house, the new school, the fresh start, more broken promises. We were still the same family, struggling with same problems, and I still had the same need to escape.

The night before I was feeling suffocated and frustrated seeing how life was creeping back to what it had always been. My dad flinging a barrage of insults, threats, and booming intimidation as we all scrambled to find the lost glasses. His lost glasses, that he wore and misplaced.

This was a normal routine for the family. I was just starting to live with them again. Maybe two months. It was like taking a wild animal into captivity, caring for it, treating it well then tossing, a fatter, more comfortable, cognizant, version back into the rough and expecting it to pick right back up on its savage ways.

Once you see what life can look like through clean glasses you can't go back to living with the dirty ones and be ok with it. You know a life that is far clearer. You can't unknow it.

As the tossing, agitation and volume of his presence grew, I stopped looking for his glasses and just asked, "Why are you screaming at us for something you lost? We can help but you don't need to act like this". I said with calm and confidence.

"Yeah, it's true" tremors of surprise radiated through me as I registered my mom saying these words. She had never stood up to him before, not like this.

My dad was speechless, eyes wide and jaw agape scrambling to find words in response to the treachery I had committed.

Regaining his composure, through gritted teeth he seethed, "Find

them now!"

We all got back to work, searching for the missing glasses. He approached me later that night about talking back and we fought back and forth, me for basic respect and him for unquestioning obedience.

We weren't his dogs.

It was all creeping back. The fresh start was already falling apart.

Upset I snuck out and walked over to my friend's house down the road. I needed to get out, get some fresh air. The long, snowcovered country road was a good escape from the hot coals brewing at home. Two kilometers away, I sat in the warmth of my friend's home, talking, sharing a smoke, as we hung out with her family and pressed tobacco into the cigarette press.

Calmed down and feeling cheerful again, I went back home. My parents were gone to work to clean offices. All the doors were locked. I went around the house looking for a way in. I was not staying in the pig barns. I tried knocking to see if my little brothers would open up. Nothing. I broke in the back patio held by a small eye hook. I slunk into my room to find it locked. I slept in the basement that night on the stock shelves.

I woke up and went upstairs to face my consequence. My mom was furious and was grounding me for life. She sent me to grab the things from the attached granny flat on the opposite side of the house, as the oldest I got to have that space. With my behaviour I would be staying in the guest room in the main house.

I gathered my things, packing them into a box, I saw my dad coming from the barn as I looked through the granny flat living room window. I tried to stay calm. I knew I was in trouble. Act normal. With the box in my hands, heading to the main house to my new room, he came in through the door at full force like a freight train. Knocking me and my things to the floor. Grabbing me by the hair and pulling me up to my feet.

"Who do you think you are?" he roared.

He slapped me hard across the face. I fell to the couch nearby. He twisted my arm and yanked me back up, screaming and hurling insults.

As spit flew in his fury, I remembered how he had hollered and degraded my aunt and uncle who he had hired to help in the cleaning business. They were running late; I remember how the spit splattered on the car window.

Shoved and thrown to the wall, angry fists hit my sides. "Fucking bitch, fucking useless bitch. You are out of here."

I gathered myself and ran to my room to hide and get away from his rage. He threw shoes, a book that clipped me just under my eye sending a wave of pain that left me shocked. I crumpled to the floor and shielded myself. Trying to make myself small and I sat there and cried.

Finally satisfied he left and returned with a large duffle bag that he threw on my bed.

"You are out of here. I don't care where you go but you are out of

here." He yelled, stomping his way back to the main house.

My hands shook as I packed trying to breathe and figure out what to bring, moving slowly in a daze.

Minutes later fueled by another wave of anger he grabbed me and my bag and shoved me out the front door.

Beep, Beep. No answer. Times up. Here I am standing in the snow, awaiting my sentence, with a duffle bag at my feet. He walked past me and slid into the car.

"Do you have any money?" He barked as he clipped his seatbelt into place.

"No", I said, incredulous at the absurdity of the question.

He nodded ok and then drove away, leaving me and my duffle bag at the bus terminal with no idea what to do next.

Was it because I stood up to him? What happened to "Your family will always be there?" What happened? How did this go so wrong so quickly? What's wrong with me? Doesn't he love me? How can he just leave me here? What am I supposed to do now? I wasn't quite 16.

Chapter 3 – The Lesson of Contrast

As hot is to cold, black is to white, up is to down, contrast shows us where we are in the world. It informs our preferences and gives language to the experience. How can I know something is "right" without understanding what "wrong" looks like?

How can I know gratitude for what I have if I have always had everything and more? How can I appreciate the kindness of another if I have no experience being treated otherwise? How can we appreciate what we have when we have always had it?

A family I admired welcomed me into their celebrations and get-togethers. The eldest daughter, my friend, often complained bitterly at the intrusion of her mother, her embarrassing, possessive nature. She would say how irritated she was with her mother. I listened empathetically while inside I was churning, you have no idea how lucky you are. I wish I had a fraction of what you had. I looked at her through my experience but maybe I'd feel the same if I were looking through her glasses.

The contrast shows us the different sides of life. My earliest memory with my father, one of the last ones. So different. Joyful and connected. Vengeful and punishing.

It felt as if we were living a double life. One bright, playful, and full of laughter. The other dark, cruel, and forceful. Never knowing what kind of day, it would be, you learned to start fresh each day and hope for the best.

I learned to read energy and was hyper-aware of facial expressions and tones, so conditioned to expect the worst I didn't realize I was reading people wrong. Run and hide away. You'll be safer there.

My parents' contrast.

Nicaragua, hot weather year-round, two seasons, humid and rainy, hot and dry. Canada, four seasons, Snow and ice, warm temperate springs, hot summers, and cool refreshing falls.

Spanish. English.

LIVING WITH DIRTY GLASSES
Dictatorship. Democracy.

A community. Isolation.

Macho. Liberal.

Traditional. Modern.

The adage is "we don't know we have until it's gone". Contrast can be painful. It can be ugly but equally beautiful. As an artist, contrast is what makes art interesting. It makes life interesting, though not easy.

Our experiences are much like the seasons. Some warm and inviting and others long, cold winters, desolate and unforgiving.

Contrast is what makes the experience.

We cannot truly appreciate one without the other.

The greater the contrast,
the greater
the potential.

Great energy
only comes from
a correspondingly
great tension
of opposites.

Carl Jung

Chapter 4 – What Is Divorce? … Mama? Wait

A child's secret prayer for divorce.

Playing outside on a cool spring morning, my 7-year-old self is hanging off the railing of the school yard stairs. I am spinning and hanging upside down at recess on my own, imagining the people I'll perform for one day. I'll show them the greatness of my bar-spinning tricks. I am lost in the depths of my imagination, the cheers, the applause. I am pulled away from my fantasies to the sound of sniffling, a stifled moan.

Who could possibly be sad during this epic performance? The weeping pulls me out of my show and I seek out where they are coming from. I see my classmate, Melissa, eyes shrink, wrapped in tears, crimson and puffy.

"Melissa! What's wrong?" I ask

She blurts out, "My mom and Dad are getting a divorce" and succumbs to heavy sobs.

I crouch down beside her on the concrete hill and put my arm around her.

"What's a divorce?" I ask stupidly.

Blubbering through her tears, she chokes out, "it's…when. Your …mom and …dad don't live together anymore" - more tears. I gave her a hug. I was surprised and wasn't sure what to say so I just hugged her and thought about what she had told me.

Lying in bed that night I was inspired by the idea. I wondered why she would be so sad about it. As I grew up, I remember holding the thought that, if only they were not together, our life would be so much better. Dad wouldn't be so angry all the time. Mom wouldn't be so sad all the time. The yelling, the fights, the cries for help, the keeping us away from Grandma and aunt Mariam, most recently making mom cry on her birthday, coupons for Burger King in hand.

I could see that my parents were very different people when they were together than when they were apart. There was time in between storms when things were calm. Like just after an eruption, they would only exchange necessary information and avoid one another. Yet, with my younger brother and I they were more engaged. Perhaps time with us kids was a distraction. Either way, the extra attention and connection was always welcome, even though the tension between them was thick.

During these times, they were always more patient, played card games with us, took us out to play ball and toss pop flies, go for drives and play at the park or, my favorite, a sleep over at grandmas. We'd have all sorts of fun.

It was the time between the storms that was my favorite. There was a calm in the air. Sad smiles replaced tears and screams. The lead up to the storms were the worst. You felt it coming on well before the drop of pressure and rain blankets the skies.

Pressure would build and flood our spaces. You had to tread carefully to not set off the tsunami of emotion pent up and pulsing to find its escape. When it did, we would be summoned from our cartoons, with cries for help, screams, tears. Keys taken, money locked in a safe, the key for the computer taken to work. The threats. Forcing Mom to go to work when she was fevered and sick.

I saw it. "NOOOO!!! DON'T!!!. I screamed and ran screaming and
sobbing stuffing my face into the pillows. Burying myself with my teddy bears, letting them absorb my tears.

They both denied it. I know what I saw. They didn't want me to tell. They didn't want me to say a word. What happened in this house was our business. Like the locked bathroom door.

Saturday morning cartoons, Shera and the team is having an epic battle. My brother and I are slack-jawed, faces frozen in front of my parents' bedroom tv. It's cold and wet outside, that time when slush and snow make for wet boots and a dampness that creeps right into your bones.

An alarm goes off. No one can hear it but me.

There is shuffling down stairs. I hear it but ignore it, Shera's battle is way more interesting. In my short years, I've learned to stay out of the

LEAH SPELT LIGIA
crossfire. Hide and make myself as small as possible. Seek cover and let it pass.

My stomach is churning. I'm getting that feeling. I ignore it. I'm just going to stay here with my brother and enjoy the show.

Bang. Bang. Bang.

My heart starts racing. Stay. Stay here.

Bang. BANG.

Bang. Bang.

Stay. Don't move.

My Dad calls me to come down. I freeze. All the hairs on the back of my neck rise as a cold trickle of fear slides down my back. I don't want to move but I know better than to ignore the call.

"Ligia Elena, come here!" he commands.

I tell my brother, "I'll be right back I'm going to get us a snack."

My Dad is pacing back and forth. A phone in one hand, a pen in another. "Ligia! Open!", he yells at my mom as he pounds on the bathroom door.

He sees me there, stops.

"Tell your mom to come out, tell her to open the door."

He sticks the pen in his mouth trying to remove the outer casing.

I press my ear to the door.

"Mama? What's wrong?" I ask

I can hear the familiar sounds. My mom is crying. I can hear her face stuffed into her arms. I can almost feel her heaving through the door. I've sat with my mom through her tears, stroking her hair, offering comfort as her heart splintered, trying to navigate the chaos our life had become.

I feel panic rise in my belly. Something's wrong. Something is very wrong. My eyes start burning. "Mama, please open the door."

"Mama! open the door. Mama! let me come in. Let me help you. Mama! What happened?" Her cry sounds different. A surge of urgency and fear engulfs me as I continue to plea with her.

Dad is on the phone talking to someone. I start crying asking her please to open the door. "Let me come in." I want nothing but to feel the warmth of my mom, to smell the sweet fragrance of her perfume and have her tight-permed curls tickle my nose.

"Mama!" I slap on the door. I know something is terribly wrong, I don't know what it is but I just want to get through this door to mom.

We cry together.

"Mama?"

Seeing my mom won't open the door for me, he hands me the phone. I hear the operator say they are on their way as he attempts to pry the door open. He's talking to her but I hear nothing... I can feel my dad panicking.

He sends me upstairs, ignoring my question, "Why won't mom come out?"

I can't imagine a world with you gone. I'd be lost without you. What demons are you fighting? I will fight them with you, just let me in.

Mama please don't leave me. Can't you hear me? Please don't leave me.

Just let me in.

I just want to hug her to be there to hold her and tell her I love her. I need her.

I returned to the show, hugged my brother and told him everything was ok, he's 3 years old and oblivious, so caught up in his show. I try to watch, but the magic of the show is gone. How could I pay attention between the banging, the pacing down stairs, the commotion in my heart? The front door is opened. Cool air rushes in. The whirl of sirens comes closer.
LEAH SPELT LIGIA

I look through my brother's bedroom window that faces the front of the house. An ambulance was parked out in front, in front of our house. Heavy footsteps stomp through the doorway and shake the house. I look back at my brother and hold him close telling him he has to stay with me. He plays with his cars and I take another peak out the window.

Time crawls. I finally see my mom. Two ambulance men are holding her up while they walk her down the path. I can see her shaking as they walk her to the back of the ambulance. She can barely stand up. From the second-floor window, I can see her whole body shaking. They put her in the ambulance and drive away with my mom.

Mama, where are you going? Please don't go. I'm praying. Don't let go. Mama, I still need you. Don't leave me here alone.

In writing this now, I realize how desperate she must have been. How desperate she was for help. How trapped she felt. She made her pain physical. In need of outside help, she wouldn't open the door until the paramedics were there and they threatened to break down the door.

Once the ambulance left, my dad packed us up and we went to the hospital, only hearing the soft chatter of the radio.

We sat in a windowless room waiting at the hospital. I sat cross legged picking at the faded edges of the linoleum floor, leaning on the brown paneling of the walls. Cushions covered in a thick, old avocado green vinyl - cracked and splitting, many bottoms sitting, waiting, praying. A man with clear framed glasses, a head above my dad, a crown of sandy blonde hair, came in. I was busy looking at the many dots and speckles of grey, brown and gold in the worn floor tiles.

"They took you away on a table

I pace back and forth as you lay silent and still.

They hook you up to feel your heartbeat.

Can you hear me? "Mama, please don't go…"
Silence… a long monitor beep, beeeeeeep, rushing, a burst of commotion as they try to undo what she has done.

On the ride to the hospital my mom's heart stopped, the doctors said. They were trying to bring her back. The medication had too much time, they told us, her heart was failing to restart. We should prepare for what happens next. If they can restart, they are unsure of the damage. If they can't…

What do they mean?

What did you do?

Why are you going to leave me?

Mama! Why?

These questions race through my mind. Stay quiet. Stay small.

The minutes ticked by, feeling like hours.

Mama don't let go.

Mama don't leave me here.

Please, Mama.

I prayed the only way I knew how.

Abuelita, always held me and we'd pray to the angels to keep us safe. Sweet angels, please don't take my mom away from me. The edges of my world felt grey. I felt so alone. I wanted my Abuelita, she'd know what to do.

Life is a balance of
holding on
and letting go...

Chapter 5 – Dandelion Dreams

As the hours stretched on, I fell asleep and dreamed of dandelions, wishing for spring to return soon. I needed them now more than ever.

I close my eyes, I'm back home - before we moved. When I used to step out of the apartment door complex, on one side I had a forest that separated the high-speed city road, with logs to climb, mushrooms to find, and delicious blackberries to nibble on. On the other side and behind the apartment buildings, were wide open fields. This was my playground.

I'd walk, arms outstretched, in the fields, brushing my hands through the tall grasses, the sun warm on my face, lost in dreams of faraway lands of magic and enchantment.

A drifting dandelion seed wisps across my nose. I watch it floating, spinning, slowly dancing along with the current of the breeze. For a moment, time is suspended. Nothing else is there.

Abuelita, once told me that dandelions hold our dreams. Dandelions are the best of listeners. They take our wishes to where they need to be, to a place where they are planted to come true.

I had to catch my dandelion. I had to make my wish. I had to tell it. I had to tell it the thing I wished most.

A breeze picks up, tickling my ears, I reached out to catch the little wonder in my hands.

The chase was on. Climbing, following, jumping, crawling, running up a rock taking a leap, and falling into the bed of grass and flowers. As I look up, dandelion fluffs are floating everywhere.

Small plump hands clasp around the delicate seed and I cup it close to my chest not believing my luck. This seed was sent to me. In a breathless fervor, I breathe hot into my palms whispering the very thing I want the most. "I want to be just like you, flying, to dance amongst the breeze, twirling in the soft current".

Looking down I see my hands are empty. The spell is now broken. I look up and reach, hands grasping only to send it in a tailspin, driving it further away. Deflated as I watching floating away.

Bring mama back home to me, please, I send up my whisper, my plea.

A little bit parent

A little bit teacher

A little bit
best friend

And a little bit
partner in crime

Chapter 6 – My Fairy Godmother's Name Was Abuelita

I strapped on my red patent leather shoes and we took our ride to the theater. It was so elegant and enchanting. I was mesmerized by the high ceiling, the chandeliers that sparkled and moved above us. My face mirrored the luxurious red carpet as and the doorman - dressed in a wonderful suit, with gloved hands and a cylindrical hat affixed to the top of his head, held the door open for me, escorting me inside as is tipped his hat.

I felt like I had walked into the scenes from Beauty and the Beast. A central staircase split off at the landing, one leading to the right of the theatre the other to the left.

I could hardly move at that moment. I felt like I had walked into a dream - a dream where wishes do come true. I was surrounded by beautiful women and classy men dressed in sharp tuxedos.

Abuelita surprised me with tickets to a special night out. A gift just for me. We had tickets for one of the most popular and talked about productions at the time, Andrew Lloyd Webber's production of The Phantom of the Opera, at the Princess of Wales Theatre in Toronto.

She didn't just take me to the theatre. It was the event of my life. Grandma pulled out all finest she had. She made me a dress especially for this occasion - a pale pink dress. Knee-length, layers to exaggerate the bell. A long lace v-front with delicate ribbons, that ran over to the other side. Long sleeves, ruffled cuffs, and a beautiful white sash to tie in a bow across my middle.

She took the afternoon to bathe me, fix my hair, and paint my nails. Just a slight hint of a sweet perfume, a matching necklace. She surprised me with a gorgeous warm dress coat, white gloves, and a little purse to hold my lip chap and candy.

It was a dream come true - the performance and the coffee and treats after. My Abuelita always let me drink milk coffee, extra milk, and a scoop of sugar.

Cinderella, Cinderella, CINDER-ELLL LA!

Out of all the Disney princesses, Cinderella was my favorite. She displays strength and faith despite the challenges and difficulties of her life. Always excluded, and treated as less than dirt, the endless workload put on her shoulders, she carries on with her work with a peaceful heart as if she holds a secret that keeps her centered. She refuses to let her circumstances make her bitter or resentful like those who she serves. She conveys kindness and is thoughtful. She is caring with all the little creatures, who repay that kindness with gratitude. They help her get through her endless list of chores. My favorite part of that movie is when she gets a visit from her fairy godmother.

Abuelita was my saving grace, my real-life fairy godmother. She gave me a home base. She let me know there was a whole other world outside of what we were living. She gave me examples of what love looked like, felt like, love that my mom was too broken and unable to give. She demonstrated patience and generosity in judgment that my dad was too agitated and under pressure to comprehend. She was a safe place. I could leave my fear at the door and just be...free. Every time it was time to put that heavy, stifling suit of fear back on, I would cry. To leave felt like being sentenced. I was desperate to stay with her, with my aunt and uncle, who lived there too. As a whole, they made it feel like home. There was nowhere I would rather be.

There, I learned that life could be happy. Laughter. Playfulness. A life that didn't have the daily heartache. No threat of rage and tension. A world away from fights, cries for help, the heavy welts, the hits of fury, and broken things.

Her fierce love, endless acceptance and encouragement calmed my fears. She held me through the thrashing, the screams, when I fought in my sheets on nights I stayed over. Another nightmare. She knew what was going on, yet she felt powerless to stop it. She gave me all of her.

She was a young single mom of 4. My Mom is the oldest. She came to Canada, as a single mother for a new start. My aunts and uncle were 18, 14, and 8. They had very little money and were all working, trying to make enough to live and go to school, while learning English.

She managed to save up enough Zellers points to get me a Sesame Street kitchen. I loved that bright green kitchen. For my birthday, she always made me a birthday dress or outfit. She was a seamstress by trade. A bright royal blue dress shirt with red stitching, a white patterned skirt, red patent shoes complete with delicate ruffles and white socks folded just so, was one of my favorites. I always felt like a princess around her. She swept my hair from my face in a neat bun with a ribbon that matched what I was wearing.

She never added to my shame. At night, before we went to bed, we would pray together. "Angelito de mi guardia, dulce compania, no me desamparaes ni de noche ni de dia, Con dios, me acuesto. Con dios, me despierto en la luz an amor del espirito santo. Amen." We'd fall asleep talking about all the things we were grateful for.

Some mornings we'd wake up and the bed was wet. I would look at her wide-eyed and horrified. How could I do this at Abuelita's house!

She'd see my look on my face and quickly jump in "No, no, it wasn't you. In the middle of the night when we were sleeping so snug, the ceilings opened up and it rained. That is why the bed is wet. Pepita, you have done nothing wrong. We cannot help when the ceiling stretches wide open and it decides to rain."

I knew it was a lie, but if it made Grandma feel better and let me save face, I was happy to go along. She sewed together the tattered pieces of my dignity, reinforcing the seams to give me strength and courage, lining my heart with extra padding to preserve the innocence and gentle spirit of youth.

In her later years, as her memory started to change and dementia started walking her through the past, she relived her time with me. She broke down and cried about the way she just wanted us to feel loved, to keep us safe, and how powerless she felt. Powerless to say anything for fear of being cut out. She focused on the best possible relationship she could give, her most precious asset – her time, her undivided attention, and her presence. She wept about how it broke her heart to see me struggling. She was sure my long bed-wetting career was due to how my dad treated me and his fits of rage. She was always there. I could tell Abuelita anything.

When I stayed with Abuelita, we would visit her friends and have tea and chat. She would take me to work at Tuxedo Royale where she was a seamstress and did alterations of tuxes. I would go around the factory and visit with the other workers who all knew me as Chiquita Banana's Grandbaby. We'd chat, I'd help them if they let me. I had my desk and chair to make clothes for my stuffed puppy friend that I took everywhere. Abuelita would give me instructions and I would work away sewing his suit. She was my biggest fan, guide, and confidant.

At her house, I'd play with her jewelry. She had accessories for every outfit. A collection of hand and feet lotions that would leave me smelling sweet and clean. Avon's Fancy Feet was my favorite. I loved the cool sensation it left on my soles, the way it tickled in between my toes, and how it turned my rank sandal smelly feet into perfumed wonders.

I'd watch her intently as she applied her makeup. I'd stare in wonder at the array of soft pencils that would bring out the texture and shape of her eyebrows, a subtly dark pink lip liner that would pull out the pout in her thinning lips.

She had a small brown flat mole on the right side of her face, just under her nose. I asked her what that was. "It's my beauty mark," she said, flashing a brilliant smile.

My Mom was often missing her eyebrow pencil as I had it hidden away to draw on my own beauty mark.

I wanted to be just like her – elegant, graceful but not too prudish to have a laugh and have some fun.

I relished her hair routine most of all and how she teased volume into her hair. She always had short hair, with a multitude of rich auburn and golden hues of sunshine, a touch of burnt sienna – all beautifully complimentary. Her hair never lay flat against her head. No, it rose to all occasions. Gooped, tussled, curled, and managed with the hairdryer to create the scene of hair full of volume, style, and "oomph". Sometimes, during the procedure, I'd have to stifle a laugh because her hair would look like she stuck her tweezers into the electrical socket.

After the ordeal, she always looked like she was ready for the red carpet at an opening event.

Being an avid Disney fan, I held tight to the idea of:

"Holding a dream your heart makes. In these dreams, you lose your heartache. To hold faith, no matter how your heart is grieving, just keep believing that dream will come true." Disney's Cinderella

In any hero's journey, they come to a point where they see no way out, no solution to their quest. It's the point when they are broken, beaten, betrayed, and have just about lost all hope. There is always a small miracle, a memory, a glimpse into what could be that gives them strength and resolve to keep going the extra step.

I had always felt so out of place. At home. At school. Here I saw what could be, how I could feel - so alive and enchanted. Abuelita always exuded confidence and a default of belonging, always finding a way to connect with anyone.

Abuelita's memory is fading now as dementia short circuits her mind, working in loops, asking the same questions, and making the same comments.

Her humor remains intact, though the filter of socially appropriate resembles those of a 4-year-old. Her mannerisms, pride in her family, and fierce love stay.

I wish I could tell her what it meant to me, but I guess now the only way for me to do that is to live my life through the lens of how she looked at me and pass on that same gift to my children and those I come into contact with. I carry her presence in the way I make my coffee every day, black and just a splash of milk, just like her. The way I eat my potato skins and all the skins because she told me that's where all the nutrients were. When I indulge in a donut, it's always an apple fritter because no other tastes as sweet. The way I catch myself slouching and snap to sit upright because she always said if I wasn't careful, I'll end up hunchbacked.

Much like Cinderella, these tender moments gave me something to hold on to when I felt I would shatter. It's what gave me the strength and courage to follow my heart. It is what I kept protected all these years that allowed me to preserve gratitude and joy, to always look for the bright side, and even though I temporarily lost sight of that for a while. I found my way back. Thank you. Thank you for seeing the best in me when all I saw was everything that was wrong with me. Thank you, Abuelita. May your legacy continue to pass on, to always see the light in another.

HOLY GUARDIAN
ANGEL,
**MY SWEET
COMPANION,**
DO NOT FORSAKE ME
DURING THE NIGHT
OR DURING THE DAY
WITH GOD
I REST
WITH GOD
I WAKE
WITH THE **LOVE**
AND **LIGHT** OF THE
HOLY SPIRIT
AMEN

Chapter 7 – What Do You Mean?

Shaken awake, bright florescent lights sear my eyes. My neck is sore from being slumped over on the hospital chair. I blinked to see the shadow before me. Abuelita! What was she doing here? We left the hospital, without Mom? The doctors managed to get her heart started, they told us she was in critical care but stable for now. I didn't see my mom that day. I was safe though. Abuelita was staying over.

As I got older, I overheard Abuelita talking about that day. How I had told her everything the second we were alone. Dad trying to open the door, the ambulance, Mom walking funny, Mom's heart stopped.

Abuelita went to stay at the hospital with Mom.

My Dad took my little brother, 3 at the time, and me out for lunch at Burger King. I think he was trying to explain what happened. We were quiet and still. Dad droned on. I don't remember details of what he said but I do remember he was talking my mom down, he was telling detailed things about their marriage I didn't understand distasteful things about Abuelita, my uncle, and my aunts (all my mom's family). "Your aunt is gay; she has no respect for a marriage between a man and a woman. Your grandma was betrayed by her husband and now she wants to destroy our marriage." He went on about past fights, and how they had wronged him, how they had deceived him, what terrible people they were. "Your uncle said you were getting too fat, I told him you were growing"

I remember hot flashes of anger bubbling up when he did this. What did any of this have to do with anything? Why was my mom in the hospital? I didn't care what he said. I loved all those people immensely and there was nothing he could ever say to make me doubt them, or love them a half an ounce less. They never made me feel anything but loved and safe. Which was far more than I could say about him.

When we finally got to see mom, doctors had warned us. She had tubes in her nose and mouth, a respirator to help her breathe and keep her airways open. They said they had to tie her hands to the bed because she had tried to remove the life support when she regained consciousness. She was sedated to keep her calm.

When I saw her, I didn't cry; I didn't look right at her, either. I stared at her feet that were moving, slowly rubbing on one another. The respirator was loud and made me jump when it sucked back air to pump into her lungs. I followed the cords across the floor right up to the machine, it came to an absurdly large tube that was taped to her mouth. Another much smaller tube was also fixed to her nose, in the right nostril. I looked at her hair, it was disheveled and limp. A contrast to the lively ringlets she usually wore.

Mom's hair was always joyously full and curled with a perm and the dazzle of boxed high-lighting kit complete with cap. I avoided her eyes. I was too afraid to see, to feel what she felt.

I brought my gaze back to the bed.

Beep. Beep. Beep.

The heart monitor rang out tracing her heart rhythms. I held on to her bedside posts. The cold metal felt sharp against my skin. I moved my hand to the blanket nearby. I found myself touching something cold and smooth. I jerked back my hand, only to realize it was my mom's hand. Pale, with a slight tinge of yellow, color and life almost completely drained. Her wrists were marked and scratched. Strips of cloth wrapped around too tight. I wanted to loosen them. Why was she tied up?

I stared at the cloth that bound her wrists, I imagined my mom in an epic struggle. Yanking out IVs, lifelines, wires, all these tubes attached to her trying to keep her alive. Alarms wailing. Sirens and lights flashing. Doctors and nurses converging on her. Her chest writhing in the agony of defeat as she is strapped down to the bed. Forcing her to endure recovery.

Why was she fighting? Why was she here? If you are sick, don't you want people to help? My 7-year-old mind wondered about so many things.

What happened? Why was she so sick? How long would she be here? Why had she locked the door?

Biting my bottom lip, I inched my gaze up towards her face. Not asleep but not there either, her eyes were lidded, vacant and glossy, fixed on a distant corner of the room. I sat down on the stool by her bed. I stroked her cold hand. She flinched at my touch this time. I looked
LEAH SPELT LIGIA
up at her face. The light caught on her cheek, a fat tear rolled down, followed by another, and another.

The beeping quickened beside me, startling me out of my thoughts. My stomach started churning what was happening? I could see her chest heaving. A deep rumble in her throat spilled out. I jumped up. She started to squirm, and struggle against the restraints. Her body stiffened and jerked. A chill ran through my bones. I suddenly felt so cold. Abuelita tried to comfort her, talk to her, tell her she was safe. Alarms went off, staff responded. The nurses asked us to leave.

Late that night, when the crescent moon hung bright and low in the sky, I had my window open to let the cool night air brush the heat off my cheeks. Sleep felt far and distant. I would look up at that sky and imagine the Cheshire cat, from Alice in Wonderland, was up there smiling down at me with that mischievous smile. I'd imagine playing with him, running through the impossible forest of Wonderland. "Where can I find the cake to eat, to make me grow? I want to go far away from here, to play in Wonderland. The King of Hearts has killed my mother."

I pulled off the window screen and climbed out on to the roof, the fresh winter breeze slapping my cheeks. I'd climb to the top of the house and wish upon every star I could see. Our family's favorite song, by the Barenaked Ladies, was running through my mind… "If I had a million dollars…" I'd buy the most colorful flowers I could find, and fill every space, so she wouldn't be so sad.

Commotion pulls me out of my fantasies. I peek into my
brother's room on my way to the stairs. He is still in bed. Loud voices creep up the stairs. Mom is not even here. What is going on? I hear my dad's booming voice. I can't make out who he's talking to. Is mom home? She couldn't be. Curiosity almost gets the better of me. Then, I hear it. The unmistakable voice of Abuelita, but it sounds foreign, angry, and forceful. "Sos un monsto Alan. How you control my daughter has driven her to this. She had no other escape… Sos un Monstro."

I slunk into the space where the railing begins, to hide in the shadows and make my escape undetected if someone were to come up the stairs. I listened. I hear her fuming and accusing. She was standing up to my dad in a way no one else dared. We were all too scared. I hear her blaming him. I hear why mama is in the hospital, she tried to poison herself.

LIVING WITH DIRTY GLASSES
How do you even do that? Wait! Did Mama want to leave? Forever? Why would she leave us here? Why would she leave me? Forever? Did she want to die? She doesn't want to live? That's why?? That feeling was etched in my heart.

As a child, when you try to make sense of your world you fill in the gaps with stories that fit into your understanding. Just a few months earlier a cousin had passed. We were waiting in the car with mom while my dad went to see the family.

"What if I put ice in cousin's pants?!" my brother challenged,
making us both giggle.

"Even if you put them in a whole bath of ice, when you die you
go to sleep forever and never wake up," my mom explained.

Everyone saw it. Over the years in my teen and young adult life, I heard stories of people trying to help my mom, of giving her books so she would wake up to what was happening. People trying to talk to my dad, to reason with him, would swiftly be extracted from our lives. My dad's own family made comments about how he treated my mom. Yet every time someone got involved, he locked her down more and more. An insufferable long time passed before we would see my mom's family again. He said they were undermining their relationship.

Mom and dad went to therapy after my mom recovered enough from her suicide attempt. My brother and I were invited to two therapy sessions with our parents in the room and the therapist. He asked if we had anything we wanted to share, anything that we were struggling with. He asked how things were going at home. Did we have any questions?

Nope! I didn't know this guy, and if I said the wrong thing, who knows what could happen. This man was cold, bald, and smelled funny. Now they were on the same team I wasn't sure what would happen.
This all felt too weird.

Did he want me to tell him how sad I was that my mom wanted to leave me, leave us? Did he expect me to say I couldn't sleep at night because I kept seeing my mom in the hospital with tubes in her mouth? Or all the dreams I had of mom dying is horrible graphic ways? Did he want me to say I was even more scared when she wasn't around? She kept me safe from Dad. I didn't understand any of what was going on. I
LEAH SPELT LIGIA
didn't want to know. I just wanted to get the hell out of there and out of the spotlight.

I was going to play dumb as I did about Santa Claus. I wouldn't
show my hand.

They concluded that, after my mom's attempt and cry for help, we kids came through it unscathed and adjusted normally. I didn't buy any of it. I just wanted to run away from it all and go to my grandma's where the world made sense, where I felt safe and like I mattered.

My mom recovered and we never talked about what happened or why it happened. Life resumed as if nothing happened. The fights calmed for a while. Phrases like "it takes two to tango" became regular reminders every time my brother and I fought.

I turned inward. Drowning out the world in lyrics and music was my refuge, where I found meaning dissecting their stories, singing the chords that sang mine. Music became my way to put words to how I was feeling.

63

HOW DO YOU RUN FROM WHATS INSIDE YOUR HEAD?

THE CHESHIRE CAT- ALICE IN WONDERLAND

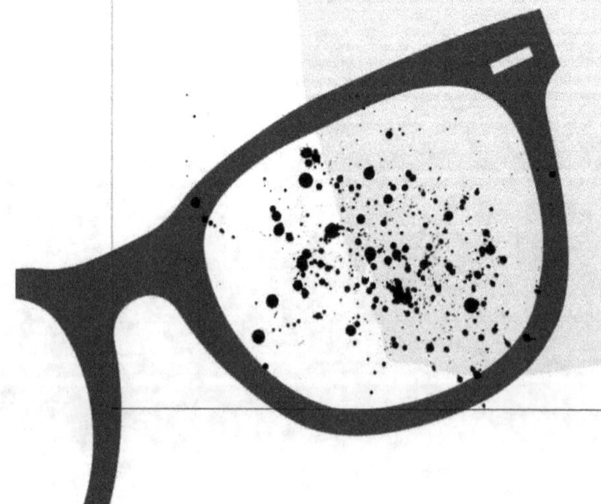

Chapter 8 – The Threat of Anxiety

Grey clouds cast across the sky. Lazy drops slide down the windshield as I drive towards the community center across town. It's been an uneventful morning. Wild berry oatmeal for breakfast with a glass of milk and banana slices. Dishes cleaned up, me and my girl dressed. I even got to her combed and parted, carefully ponytailed in position while she watched cartoons. It is our day to go to playgroup. Time to chat with other moms and swap stories of the latest milestone reached, sleepless nights, and the torture of teething, all while the kids experiment with glue and paper, run wildly in the gym, crash cars, and live in a world of make-believe.

My daughter is strapped into her car seat. A drizzle in the sky and the cool breeze whispers, as I check over the diaper bag for snacks and wipes before tossing it in the back seat. The radio plays softly in the background. My 3-year-old is humming along to childhood songs.

Somewhere between the last stop sign and passing the school I am increasingly aware of the tension in my body. My hands are aching, I didn't realize I was holding the steering wheel so tight. A boa constrictor has snuck into my car and wrapped its coils around my chest, tightening with every inhalation, causing my breath to get short and rapid.

Bees are racing through my veins, crawling under my skin. My stomach churns and rolls. I try to stay focused on the road, I feel panic rising as I'm not sure what's going on or why.

My head is pounding, louder and louder, I feel tears rise like heat being released into a hot air balloon. Flushed with heat and yet so cold I'm shivering, all at once. I pull over, put the car in park, and crumple into my hands trying to stifle my sobs as I crank the music.

"Do what you can, with what you have, where you are"
-        Theodore Roosevelt

What's wrong Mommy? My little one asks from the back seat.

"Mom just needs a minute."

"Are you sad?"

"Maybe a little. Will you sing sunshine for me? I love when you sing that song."

As my little girl sings her favorite song, I take deep breaths to gather my composure.

What the hell was that? I scold myself. What's wrong with you?

It's been happening more lately. The tight chest, the wash of overwhelm, the tears that come out of nowhere. Nothing happened. We had a great morning. What's wrong with me?

I could have just brushed it aside to say it was just hormones, I was pregnant with my son at the time. Being emotional is a normal part of pregnancy, right? With the changes in hormones and body adjustments, but this was different. I didn't experience this in my first pregnancy, but I knew the feeling.

These episodes had been happening again and again, at times with more frequency and intensity than others. Sometimes with pictures from the past that flashed through my mind, my body reacted as if it was happening again.

After that episode, I had to figure out what was going on with me and find a solution. I couldn't bring another life into this world and be the mother I wanted to be to my children while trying to hide and manage this. I didn't know where they came from, why they were happening or how to stop them.

I was tired of feeling out of control in my life. I couldn't handle the thought of continuing to live like this. This was the first time it happened while driving. I was grateful to have had the awareness to pull over when I felt myself spinning out of control.

Though I spent over 2 years in and out of hospitals, 8 years in one form of therapy or another, diagnosis of anxiety disorder, PTSD, deep depression, disassociation, and ADHD, I had ZERO ideas of what any of that meant. No one told me what any of these things were or why I was experiencing them. What were the symptoms? How could I prevent it? How could I stop it when it was happening? Instead, I was

LEAH SPELT LIGIA

put on medication to try and manage the outward symptoms, of stress and emotion, a way to numb and carry on.

I felt like a guinea pig, trying medication after medication, going from feeling nothing, to distracted, to so depressed it felt hard to move, to anger that bubbled up without provocation. Racing thoughts shifted to a zombie state of moving through one moment to the next. Nothing helped. In my case, the problem wasn't solved by chemicals. It was the thought processes, trying to create a structure of safety in my mind when my outside world felt unpredictable and uncertain. I was always waiting for the next calamity to hit, the next heartbreak, the next rejection, the next time I would have to pick up whatever I could carry and move again. It had been years since I had my new start and I was in a supportive and safe relationship. Why was this coming up now?

After my dad kicked me out, that was it for my medications and I learned how to live without them. Even when I got to a place where I could afford them, it wasn't an option. Though they work wonders for some people, I struggled to find balance and experienced heavy side effects. Despite this, I tried them again for 6 months after my daughter was born and I was struggling with postpartum depression. I found no relief in them and resolved to find another way. I was tired of feeling like a robot.

It worked. My resolve to find another way worked. For a while, my life settled down. I found my path and purpose as my daughter approached a year. For 2 years, things stayed balanced enough and I was managing, supported by community helpers, my husband, and friends – friends who welcomed us like family, when I had no family of my own. My childhood family was scattered and fighting their own battles to survive the next stage of their own lives.

I didn't understand what I did and what worked for those years. Maybe it was just dumb luck. As the assaults of anxiety became more and more frequent, they'd express themselves as a sudden burst of anger, tears that never wanted to stop, feeling on edge, irritable and avoidant. I tried to keep myself as busy as possible and around other people seemed to help until it didn't.

That night after the driving incident, I went to the counseling website in our city and I scrolled around on their website. I didn't know what I was looking for but I knew I needed answers and a way to figure out what was going on with me. I truly felt there was something inherently wrong with me. As I scrolled the page of workshops, a title stood out to me: "Calming the Storm Within."

That's it! I enrolled right away. I learned four very important things in this 6-week workshop.

What I was experiencing was called anxiety.

I was not alone in my struggle.

Anxiety is real and debilitating.

I had a choice.

I heard people's stories of the efforts and struggles they faced in

their everyday lives. Even thoughts of leaving their house were a trigger for some. It broke my heart to learn how many people live with this fear, so intense and intrusive every single day.

I learned what was happening inside me and I started to understand that these attacks weren't random but a result of unchecked thoughts that got away from me. I never really thought to pay attention to my thoughts. They seemed as automatic as breathing. I had never even considered it to be something to pay attention to, or that I was in control. I was equally as sad as I was hopeful. I realized that, if I was the source of this problem, I could be the solution.

I learned 6 exercises that help me feel more in control and over time stop the anxiety attacks.

Put an elastic band on your wrist and every time you have a worrying, or negative thought snap it as a way to bring awareness to your thoughts and a cue to change the thought to one that serves you. With time, you don't need the elastic anymore. This isn't about hurting yourself. It's about habit formation. When you snap the band, it's a reminder – Hey! This thought is hurting you (not in a huge way). Small hurts, worries, and negative thoughts compound overtime. Pay attention and choose a thought that empowers you.

Write down everything that worries you. Problems, worries, and stress grow so much bigger in our heads. When we take time to write them down, we can look at the problem with more perspective and gain some clarity as to what the

LEAH SPELT LIGIA

problem is. A step further would be to write down things we CAN do about the problem. Can I do anything about this? If yes, what? If no? How can I think of this differently? What can I do in this situation?

Play out the worst-case scenario, then ask yourself, "So what?" Another reason, "So what?" The idea is to get yourself in a problem-solving mode, to walk through the process and show yourself that it is something you can handle and will figure out, because you always do.

Visualize a STOP sign. Sometimes, before you can catch the disturbing thoughts it can be like a freight train running through your mind. STOP!!! I'd imagine a huge bright red and white stop sign that, like the Sylvester and Tweety cartoons, would have the power to stop the racing train in its tracks, making it halt on the spot, tearing up the tracks from the sudden stop. Stop and reframe. "What can I do right now about this?" Breathe. Anxiety plays out physically. Movement is the best way to slow down the racing thoughts and gain a shift in focus. Change the scenery, get out of the environment, get blood flow to the body. Go for a walk. Just start moving.

Move your body. Go for a walk, run, hike, put on your favourite music and DANCE freely (when's the last time you did that?) Lift weights, throw a ball, do some push-ups, jumping jacks, go outside and let the air hit your face.

Of these 6 exercises, writing and exercise have proved to be my freedom. I had over the years, stopped writing when my journals were exposed and things that I had said in the privacy of the page were made public in my family. I mean is there no sacred space?

I started to write and I became aware of how much I worried. I worried about money, my husband, my kids, … Most of all, I worried if I was enough, if I could be the mom these kids needed and deserved. I realized I had the constant thought that I would mess it all up. I had no idea what I was doing. Would my husband still love me? Where did I belong? Why did the lady look at me funny at the store? I worried about my past and people finding me out. I worried about making friends, I worried about school, about finishing and not finishing school. I worried if I was strong enough. I worried about keeping my job. I worried about the hours my husband worked. I worried about how fat I was. I worried about getting enough exercise. I worried about when my husband would leave me, not if but when. I worried constantly.

Anxiety is living in constant fear because we have lost all trust in ourselves to handle what is up next in life. It's a lack of the ability to imagine yourself being the hero. It's not a general lack of imagination because there is never shortage of dreaming of every possible scenario that could go wrong and how you can lose. I thought that, if I worried more, I'd be more prepared but instead, I found myself paralyzed with worry and I wouldn't make any decisions at all. My indecision caused more worry and pressure to make a decision. I tried to analyze the issue from every position, exhausting the pros and cons, and I found each side had equally effective arguments. I remained stuck in further rumination.

Let's stop here and take a minute to pull out the journal and write what's on your mind. How is this sitting with you? If you want to download free printable workbook you can find it by scanning the QR code or e-mail leahspeltligia@gmail.com.

A quote that Anne Frank wrote in her diary while in hiding in cramped quarters with her family and others for over 2 years (her only fault being born into a religion that, at the time, was a death sentence) resonates with me.

"I don't think of all the misery, but of the beauty that still remains. We all live with the objective
of being happy: our lives are all different and yet the same."

"Think of all the beauty still left around you and be happy. Whoever is happy will make others
happy."

LIVING WITH DIRTY GLASSES

Over the years I have seen, time and time again people, myself included, can make the best, most thought-out plans but things don't always work out how we plan. There is always another way, another solution, even if it's not the one we want. There is a lesson there.

It has been an important adage for me to remind myself: Do something.

Can I do anything about this? Action is the best source of relief. Action can be anything to take you out of the state of worry. Is it midnight and you can't do anything about the things keeping you up right then? Write it down. I keep a pen and paper with me at my bedside. It's a place to take the loop of the worry out of my mind and give it a home until I can do something about it.

Make the decision already. No matter what you choose, there will be gains and losses to both, take yourself out of the worry loop and to make up your mind. You can decide that, for better or worse, you will stand by that decision and learn from it and build your character.

What is the most generous assumption you can make about what is worrying you? Failing at school? You are understanding what does and doesn't excite you. Lost a job? An opportunity to refocus and recommit to what I really want in life. Saying goodbye to a friend? You realize how much life was enriched with that friend being a part of it. Hard childhood? You connect with your power to understand what you want and don't want in your life and build the life you want. When I stopped focusing on the challenge/problem I saw space open up for possibilities.

What if the situation is out of my control? For example, the past - can I do anything about it? No. Can I accept it? No? How would I need to look at this so I could accept it? How do you deny the facts of what happened?

Trauma is like an injury. It's not your fault that it happened but it is up to you to heal from it. Take for example a car accident, the person may have been drinking, texting, distracted in one form or another and hit you while driving. You find yourself in the hospital with broken legs, road rash and a wicked bump on the head.

That's not your fault and the person should have known better, operated with more thought to others and been more responsible. Triggering the "this never would have happened if" story doesn't change

the fact that the accident happened. Is it fair? No. Can you wish things were different? Yes, but it changes nothing. The accident happened. You need to work through the pain of learning to walk again.

Holding on to past hurts, opportunities you missed, mistakes you made, lost time will only hurt you and add to your baggage. We have enough to carry around. Why not make the load a little lighter and start treating yourself with some respect and appreciation for all you have already come through? Why not love yourself where you are and keep growing from there.

Much easier said than done. I get it, but it's a starting point. Awareness is key.

Scan Below to download your free workbook or e-mail leahspeltligia@gmail.com to get your free "*Clean your Dirty Glasses*" Workbook download and stay connected.

Paper has
more
patience
than
people

-Anne Frank

Chapter 9 – Running

I got to a point where all I thought about was running away. I thought about it again and again. It didn't matter where I went. After I lost my retainers and was too afraid to go home, the school started to get involved. I was looked at as a traitor and the tension got worse. My mom's family would tell me it was up to me because they couldn't get involved. I'm not sure what they expected me to do. I was a child. If grown adults couldn't face my dad, what chance did I have?

My parents were in the cleaning business and working all the time. As the business grew, so did the pressure. So did the spending. So did the distance and disconnect, and the fury. We saw my mom's family less and less.

When you are treated with a level of dignity and respect, with love and care, it becomes glaringly obvious to you when you are not. I was about 13 at the time. I didn't want to live like this anymore. My fantasies of running away became central to my world. I imagined a life on the other side of our pain. I imagined a life where if something happened it was not manipulated into being your fault. Gaslighting can make you feel like you are going crazy. The term, gaslighting comes from the 1944 film, "Gaslight", in which a husband manipulates his wife into thinking she has a psychological disease by reducing their gasfueled lights and telling her she is hallucinating. All his deception, in the effort to keep his murderous and conniving identity secret, made her question and doubt what she saw or felt. This is what it felt like to try and get help.

My only solution was to run away. I cried. I delayed. I avoided. As much as I wanted a better life, I loved my family. I saw the good in us. I saw who we could be, even if they were just little glimpses. I saw possible happiness, pure and light. With more tar being thrown over time, it was getting harder and harder to see it, to bring it up, to keep believing it. Hurt upon hurt upon hurt – our best version of the family was on feeble legs.

The wish to be taken away, to be discovered for talent, to save me, wasn't happening. How could it? I can't help but think, sometimes, about who I could have been if my mind wasn't consumed with surviving. I hear stories of kids building their scholarly careers because they understood that was their ticket out. In my heart, I played on the stage of performance. I entertained and amazed. We all handle our trauma in different ways.

I decided on the date. I had some money tucked away. Some stolen and more chiseled out of my black piggy bank from Nicaragua. It was made out of clay with no plug to open and release its contents safely. I loved my little pig. Having the choice of breaking it and getting the money or leaving it intact and continuing the breakage of me was too black and white for me.

I am a believer in greys. How could each of us get what we wanted without a hammer? I found a metal nail file instead and filed away at the deposit slot until I could slip at least a partial finger in to fish out a bill or wiggle out a coin. If only such a compromise could be made here.

I didn't care where I went. I just wanted to get away from here. I wasn't concerned about where I was going or what I would do. I was convinced that anywhere would be better than here. I had survived this. How much worse could "out there" be? My movie and TV education made me believe that, as the underdog, I was destined to come out ahead. I was going to go on this epic journey. I would emerge triumphant from the trials. The moments where I felt I couldn't go on, I would push through, because I knew this was the price I had to pay, so that my family would come together and heal. I was convinced that I had to do this to save my family.

It's warm for a fall day. I'm helping fold laundry and, my mom, comes out of nowhere and starts telling me that we are going to leave. I felt like my world stopped. She never said too much, often in her own head, trying to deal with our everyday walk on eggshells and minimize the damage. She had a habit of just suddenly dropping into topics without warning.

Take the day I was casually watching TV, minding my own business and my mom came in, took the remote, and shut off my show.

"Tell me what sex is. Do you know? I want to know what you know." She demanded.

I was dumbfounded, mortified, and completely lost for words. I didn't know how to talk this way to my mom. I felt like I had been holding a towel to cover my naked body and my mom came up and yanked it away suddenly. We had never talked about this before. Now, this? I felt like I had 63 marbles in my mouth. Eventually, I spat out mybeating-around-the-bush-concept of the boy thing and girl thing and hoped and prayed that would suffice. She pressed a few questions more. I answered and it seem to satisfy her sudden urge to dive into sex education at 13. I had learned it in school, in movies, from friends. I knew the basics. It was nothing I dared to discuss with my mom. It ended as abruptly as it began. I laugh at the memory now. I learned my mom didn't have any discussion with her mom about sex so this was progress.

I learned quickly this idea of leaving had been on her mind a lot. She talked to me about her plan. She shared with me her why and the life she hoped to build for me and my brother. How we would still always see our dad, that he was a good dad and that they weren't getting along. She talked about the women's shelter and what it was like. She shared with me the information she had gotten about the cycles of abuse, what it looked like, how it wasn't her responsibility to be perfect for him. He had no right to treat her that way. She talked about our plan to leave when there was a space available. I was struck by the gentleness and kindness in her voice. I was moved by the softening of the hard ridges of stress and worry around her eyes. Mom always seemed so far away.

I could feel my heart filling with hope and happiness of a new beginning of more times like these. What fortified my allegiance to this idea was that she wasn't treating me as a child, she was treating me as her confidant, her partner, her source of strength to support her through this transition, to light the way, to hold her hand. Mom was letting me in.

When I pick up the glasses my mom was wearing, I understand she had nothing to give. She was trying to survive and fight through another day. To battle between what her heart was calling her to do, to create a life for us that was so opposite to what we were living and her mind, how could she support us and how could she leave and still be safe. She wanted to be freed, she wanted us to be free.

She was always on edge. Always needing to make the house perfect. She was still trying to figure out life with the scares etched deep from her trauma, her years of living in quiet, spirit breaking desperation. They were few, but the times I remember being full of joy were when she was relaxed enough to just be with us, playing card games, having conversations and joking, watching movies together. Sometimes all you need is a little hope.

All of this came days before my decided runaway date. I would have been on the bus ride to school in the morning, carrying on just like any other day. I would have gotten off the school bus at school and made my way to the city bus and walked away. Now, none of that mattered. I needed to be there for my mom. We had a new dream we were building and we would do this together. The three of us had a path to a better life. I didn't have to do it alone... I didn't have to break away.

These were some of the best and closest times I would ever have with my mom. We talked and talked, we got along. I felt happy. She was happy. It made weathering the storms a little less damaging. We had a plan, a day that was coming that all this would stop. All this would be over. We could be a real family.

Days went by. They crawled into weeks which rolled over into months. My Mom said she was calling. She said they didn't have space yet. She said we were on the waiting list. She said she would keep calling.

After the hurricane of my dad passed one evening, I saw my mom curled up on the couch. That look had crept back into her eyes. I didn't know why or what happened but I saw it. The fear. She had the phone in her hand. She was calling again. When was this going to happen for us? When could we leave? I felt sad for my dad. Mom reassured us she wanted us to love our dad and see him often. They just couldn't live together anymore. She never wanted to take us away from him. He was, after all, a good dad, who loved us. She loved the side of him that loved her, that treated her with love and respect. She loved the man after the storms looking to make amends. She knew he was broken. She saw how he struggled, likely why she hung on to their relationship for so long. More likely, she was afraid of what he would do, afraid of his anger and vengeful nature. No doubt a slippery dance between the two. That is not my story to tell.

The air in our home had changed after that last exchange. They had been co-existing. Not fighting, not talking, just courteously passing one another and engaging more with us. Something weird was happening. I stayed, waiting for the day my mom would tell us it was time. I was praying for a spot. I had my bag packed. I was ready to start my new life.

More time passed. It seemed an eternity. One afternoon after school we came home and found our parents at the table talking. We ran upstairs to our rooms and slumped down in front of the TV. It was a long day and I wanted nothing to do with anything. I didn't worry about them talking though. We had a plan. We were leaving for a better life. This was a necessary step. A while later, somewhere between the dreamy Zack from Saved by the Bell and the dorky suspender slinging Urkele, we got called downstairs. I assumed it was time to set up for dinner. We went downstairs to the kitchen table. Dad in his usual spot at the head of the table, mom in her spot to his right. They invited us to come to sit down. I assumed my spot to the left of my dad and my brother assumed his spot opposite the head of the table. My mom started. She asked us a simple question. No preliminary. Right to the point as her style of conversation usually went.

"Are you afraid of your dad?" I was so shocked and horrified by the question being asked right in front of our dad. I felt the jagged edge of betrayal slice down my side, exposing me, revealing my secrets. Divulging the vulnerable spot in me where I kept myself hidden and strong. What was she doing?? What was this about? Why?? My brother and I had no words and almost on cue we started crying.

A recent memory flashed of my dad with my little brother sitting in his chair, red-rimmed eyes full of tears, as he watched my dad, hammer in hand, shouting that he would learn his lesson. I don't even know what he had done. I do know how hard my brother worked doing extra chores and how proud he was of finally being able to buy that watch with his own earned money. Now my dad had it on the table smashing it into pieces calling me down to bear witness as my brother looked on heartbroken.

My dad was so hurt and in disbelief with our reaction and the revelation that – yes, in fact, we were afraid of him. He muttered something about how he had respect for his mom and her discipline, but he was never afraid of her. He fought back his tears and tore away from the table leaving us there crying with my mom.

It was as if he had no idea the impact his angry fits of rage had on us, all of us. He, in his level of understanding, was right and true doing the things that were hard and necessary to do. He was giving it his best and now he was coming to find, in complete shock to him, that he was doing this all wrong. I'm not sure how that came as such a surprise to him. How do you ignore the pleas to stop? How do you not hear the cries? How do you ignore the welts and bruises? Now, he was the victim somehow. We were ungrateful slime that just looked for what's wrong in him.

After that day, I was afraid to ask but I built up the courage at home alone with Mom, "When are we going, Mom?" I asked softly.

"We aren't. They have no room. I've been talking with your dad. We are going to work this out."

"But you can still call, keep calling. Mom! You promised!" came out shrill and urgent.

"There is no room." She responded plainly and went about her work signaling to me the conversation was over.

Angry tears sprung down my face. I trusted her. I believed things would be different. I was there for her! Now, she was changing the plan and shutting me out. The indifference and avoidance felt like her reaching into my heart and squeezing the life out of it.

The hope was gone, throwing a boulder into my dreams of a different life – one where we could live together and happy, one where I could finally have Mom. A life where my mom wasn't preoccupied with surviving – mom, who was there for us, the mom I so wanted to be a part of my life.

After months of being best friends and planning and chatting together, believing with every fiber of who I was, that this was real and was going to happen, it was gone. I had felt like my continuous childhood cries and prayers were finally being answered, only to be crushed and dismissed like dandelion seeds in the wind.

I picked up my shattered pieces and took myself upstairs.

Betrayed, heart-broken, how could I trust anyone? My "best friends" would leave me, gang up on me, bully me. Home was no different. Maybe I just invited these types of people into my life. It seemed to be all I was good at is being hurt and believing in people who would only let me down.

Now what? Alone again. Color drained from my world. It didn't matter what I did, it was always wrong. I always came up short. No one saw what I saw. No one felt the truth the way I did. The tears eventually subsided. I had to move on. A thought crept into my mind, from the innermost hollow of me. A part I didn't even know.

Like a garden, the mind must be tended to. Weeds need to be pulled out, productive seeds need nurturing, watering, warmth and sun. Weeds can be invasive and consume the fertile garden.

It started with a whisper, a tiny seed of a thought, that would grow to take over my life for the next 24 months - so insidious and persistent it would not be silenced.

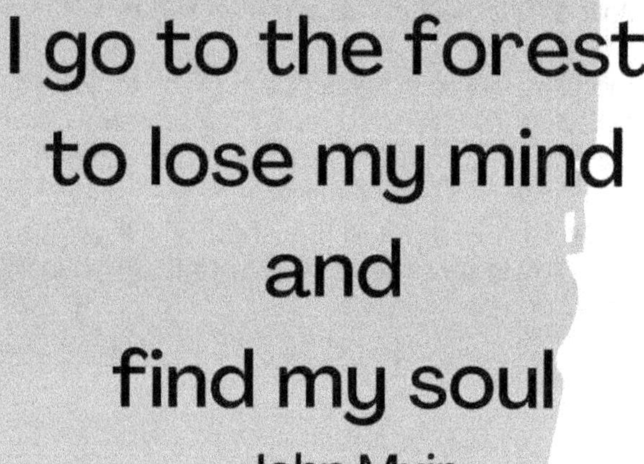

I go to the forest to lose my mind and find my soul

\- John Muir

Chapter 10 – So Close

Consciousness rolled in and out of me, my dad leaning over me, "How could you do this to me?"

"You? This has nothing to do with you" I thought as I dropped off into the darkness.

Have you ever been so bad at...well, just about everything? Do you think, "I can do this? I can't mess this one up." Only to realize even this, this too?!?

Dread slipped into my chest as realization slowly opened the curtains to my mind.

Awareness creeping in as every cell in my body felt like it had been put through a meat grinder. I took in the room around me. Wires, machines beeping, bright lights above, and that dreaded smell. The smell of cleaning products trying to mask the odor of sickness and decay. A mix of citrus and substances to cover the stench of human waste and the struggle for life.

The fog lifting slowly, hazy and hard to see.

I knew it would be unlocked. The ward was open, I knew it was now or never. I had to get out of here.

I walked towards the lunchroom door. The exit from the ward was conveniently a few feet past it. I opened the door. The staff was about 100 feet away in the nursing station, busy chatting, finishing up paperwork before the next shift started.

I slithered out the exit door. My heart pounding in my chest, hollering in my ears. I pressed the elevator button furiously. Did they see me? Would someone notice?

Would someone be there? There in the elevator? Would they know? My hands were shaking as I pressed. One. Two. Come on! Come on! I was waiting for a hand to grab my shoulder. Come on! I pressed harder imagining it might make the elevator go faster.

Ding.

The doors slid open and I slipped in, frantically searching for the close door button. Close door.

I was sure I would have been caught by now. I was sure I'd be put in the observation room, and the ward would be locked down again. I didn't care. I wouldn't be back anyway.

The door closed. My lungs ached. I released my breath all at once. I didn't realize I had been holding it.

I made my way down the corridor and went out to the hang-out spot where the kids with privileges would go to have a smoke. Thinking back, the idea that minors had smoking privileges still boggles me, though I had no trouble participating in it at the time.

I could hear CODE Yellow. My escape was just being registered and I was already out the door. I ran.

I ran and ran, my heart throbbing in my throat, yelling in my ears, I ran until my legs burned and I made it to the busy street. There was a plaza just down the road on the other side.

This time would be different I told myself. This time I would get it right. I had some money in my pocket. I prayed it wouldn't be too expensive. I made my way into the Zellers department store, the automotive section. There it was, only 3 dollars. I bought a jug of windshield wiper fluid and a Mountain Dew. I tried to slow my step to not cause alarm around me. My skin goose-bumped and my hair raised. My breath was shaky. I took a few deep breaths to steady myself, to slow it all down. I didn't want to raise suspicion.

Wiper fluid in one hand, cool bottle of pop in the other, I found a secluded spot. There in the corner of the strip mall surrounded by the walls meant to keep the huge generator protected and out of the way.

I dumped half my pop out and refilled the bottle with windshield wiper fluid.

My hands shivered. My whole body trembled with anticipation. Rivers flowed as I took my first drink. The solution burned my throat and left my mouth feeling numb and cold. I cried as I drank. I cried for my family. I cried for my mom, for my little brother who I would never see grow up. I cried because I'd never see Abuelita again. I cried for the happy memories we had had. I cried because I realized I was going to die here all alone.

I planned to make my way back to a spot by the train tracks, where the stream trickled and gurgled. Where the water was cool and comforting. There I would lay upon the grass and let nature take me home where I didn't have to feel so damned alone. I'd hear the bird's chirp. I'd feel the warm breeze caress my face and there I would lay watching the fuchsia pink wildflowers dance before I fell asleep.

Nature had always been my escape.

When tension in the house was too thick, I'd go to that place, just past the soccer fields and into the forest. I'd climb trees growing right over the river and lay there dreaming and wondering, intoxicated by the beauty all around me.

The hues of green and brown. The way the sun trickled in through the branches to nourish the plants growing along the ground. I'd sit quietly and still and watch a robin build its nest, or ants crawling to their hill. The rush of the river always brought calm to my racing heart. Here in nature, I could forget I was afraid. I could forget to pretend. I could forget I didn't belong. I was home here among the trees. I felt held and safe, calmed by instinct.

I realized too late that I hadn't calculated in my plan how fast this poison would work. Methanol, the main ingredient in windshield washing fluid, is extremely poisonous. As little as 2 tablespoons (30 milliliters) can be deadly to a child. About 2 to 8 ounces (60 to 240 milliliters) can be deadly for an adult. I had drunk ¾ of my bottle.

I got up, wiped my face. The shaking had stopped. My world became pixilated and distorted. I figured I should have my last meal before I go to the stream. All urgency evaporated. I found myself unsteady and, as I tried to make my order for a pizza slice, my words came out slurred. My world was spinning. And I was stumbling. It wasn't until I got the furrowed brow from the pizza guy taking my order that I thought, "Oh no! It's working too fast. I have to get the stream. I have to get to the stream."

After 23 attempts, 2 years in and out of hospitals, family fighting at an all-time high, my panic so loud I couldn't drown it out, drops into depression and hopelessness that the nightmare of my life would ever end, I finally got it. I finally got the right formula. I had drunk, bottles of Tylenol, cough syrup, fish tank cleaning tablets, prescription pills, pills I found at the offices we cleaned. Anything I could get my hands on to numb the pain, to make it stop, to quiet the chattering. Sometimes I was caught and the ambulance called other times I would just wake up groggy and more depressed. I just couldn't escape.

I was too skittish for blood. I was too afraid of heights and sudden impact. The anticipation would be far worse. I just wanted to go to sleep and never wake up. I didn't know that, according to a poll by Harvard Case Fatality Rates by Suicide Method, 1989–1997, only 1.5% of overdoses by ingestion of pills or poison are ever successful.

No matter what I did, I just could not get it right and I was causing more pain and heartache to my family, I became more and more convinced that I was the problem. The more it didn't work, the more I wanted to see it through.

I was trying to go quietly. I was trying to not make such big ripples in our lives I just didn't want to live. I waited long stretches and acted like everything was fine. I waited until I had collected enough pills to do it again. I didn't have much money and everything was in lockdown. I took it from my friend's house. I had tried so many times that I was kept in the hospital under observation. I missed a ton of school and eventually, it came out that they were going to send me to a Psychiatric Hospital for treatment. There would be a month's wait before a spot would be available. I wasn't in a good place at home.

I was home on weekends once in a while and this last time there was a dispute. I was oblivious with earbuds stuffed in my ears. What I do remember is the crying, the yelling, grabbing shoulders, the shoving, and finally being locked out of the house. I brought it up during a therapy session with my parents so we could deal with it and sort out what happened. My parents both looked at the therapist and me with shock and disbelief. Laughing and asking if I had been at the same house with them on the weekend. Then, with a look of utmost concern and truly wanting to understand, my dad asked if I might have had multiple personality disorder. He said that he had read that this could explain the things I was seeing. Enraged, I told them I knew what they were doing. Mom takes dad's side. Dad tells me it never happened.

I felt my rage bubble up inside me. I hated these people. Now, they were blaming the landscape of our lives and the torment of how we lived on me. They were pretending that I was delusional and inventing it for what? Attention? Gaslighting. I was indignant and heartbroken. I wanted help, I wanted us to be ok. I didn't want trouble; we were a family struggling to stay afloat.

Not long after that session, I had been informed that she attempted to take her life again. I was repelled and disgusted by her crying and telling me how sorry she was. "Yeah! I'm the problem here." I think the staff believed me after that incident. If the problem was in my head and everything else was fine, why would she do it again?

I know now the hold he had on her and the consequences she faced if she didn't go along. He threatened her whenever she hit her breaking point, he'd take her children away and use the suicide attempt as evidence she was an unfit mother. Where do you turn when your world is falling apart?

I go to the forest
to lose my mind
and
find my soul

- John Muir

WHAT YOU CAN'T SAY OWNS YOU

WHAT YOU HIDE CONTROLS YOU

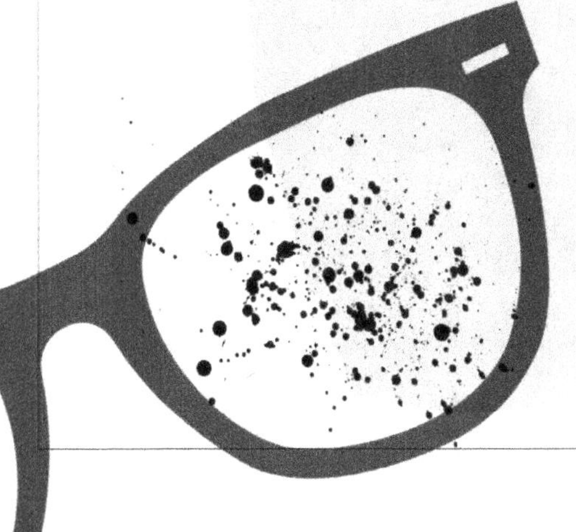

Chapter 11 – What Will You Miss? Belonging.

In school playing soccer - we were practicing our kicks. In my mind, I was going to launch it farther than anyone had ever seen. I was going to have the greatest kick. Instead of just doing the standard run up and kick like all the other kids I took several feet back and took a running kick. I lined up and ran as hard as I could swinging my right leg as far back as it would go behind me and bringing it right up to boot the ball.

What I saw next was not what I had expected. Instead of seeing my ball fly out toward the teacher what I saw was the clouds and my leg above me flailing in the sky followed by a heavy thud.

I got up, I brushed off the grass, adjusted my shorts and tee-shirt trying to soothe my pride and gave the ball a quick kick then scurried to the back of the line avoiding eye contact and snickers.

Clumsy and awkward, overweight from the prednisone I had to take to control my asthma and our Latino portion-sizing, eat-everything-on-your-plate-there-are-people-starving mentality didn't help either.

I was too loud, too brash, too much.

Making friends is never easy when you are the target of the bullying. They make fun of your hair, your four-eyed glasses, and the jam stain of a birthmark just below your lower lip that you can't rub out. Even when your parents tried to remove it with painful bi-monthly laser treatments at the Children's Hospital in Toronto. Despite the numbing cream, it felt like steel wool being rubbed over my skin to try and rub out the stubborn, shameful spot. These treatments left it deep purple and scarlet colored, and scabbed for weeks until it healed. I often hid my glasses and only wore them when necessary. They were just another thing to make me stand out. An outsider, the girl with the scar to prompt all those around her that she was not to be loved. A permanent mark to remind her she'd never fit in. Forever flawed and defective.

I didn't belong anywhere. At home I was too Canadian to be understood by my parents, to be heard. It was too dangerous to be anything but invisible.

At school, I was too foreign to fit in. Too sickly, too fat, too much of a liar (a habit I picked up very young to stay out of trouble, then adapted to try and fit in). The ironic thing is that the more I tried to blend in the more I alienated myself from my peers. How could I blame them? How do you trust a shapeshifter, a chameleon who was always changing her story? I didn't belong in their world no matter how much I tried.

I kept myself company with my imagination. It's the one thing that was always there when I was scared, when I was lonely, when I wanted to run away, when I wanted to hide from my life. My imagination and I were the best of friends until she started questioning why we were still here. Why, when there was so much pain in the world? She took me into the dark and desolate parts of my world. My smile and tenacity traded for tears and isolation.

ᴗᴗ

This moment, as I am finished choking down what I can of my freedom from this pain that has me in its grips, the pain I can't escape, that brings so much ache and hurt to my family, I think of my life. Love fills my heart. I'm not afraid. I want this all to end. I cannot bear another day to carry the lies, the betrayal, the utter loneliness and longing I feel. I want to just feel safe and like I belong somewhere.

My failed attempts to order my pizza give way to the urgency to go to the stream. The poison is too quick. I need to get to the stream. I stagger and start making my way out the door hardly able to pull it open and will my hands and feet to move in the direction I need them to. The stream is all I think of, get to the stream, pain is gripping my insides as the poison is coursing through my blood and saturating my cells.

I approach the busy four-lane highway where people are rushing home from their day jobs to be with their families. Out of the corner of my eye, I see, a police car jumping the curb and heading straight for me.

My reflexes are gone, I feel a jolt on my right leg and I fall onto the hood and land on the grass. No. No. I need to get to the stream. A flood of questions and yelling are coming at me but I can't hear a sound. I only feel the force of their words hit my face as fists are jammed into my sternum. The idea, I learned, later on, was to determine my pain response. I see people all around me but I feel nothing. I see them yelling. I see their arms shaking. I know they are rubbing into my sternum. I feel nothing at all.

The clouds look like cotton candy pulled across the light blue-colored sky. The darkness starts creeping in along the edges closing in towards the center until there is nothing more I see and I am consumed by the pitch of the night.

Exhausted from the chatter, despair pulled me down into the darkness, where the trolls hide their trinkets. Light at that time was in planning the finale. I had gone from trying to pass school to a full-time job of trying to figure out how I was going to die in the most painless way possible.

Burns and deep scratches littered my arms and legs. I craved for something to qualify my pain, something physical, something real. A broken leg we know how to repair, an infection we can deal with, a mind lost in darkness entangled in the thorns - how did I get here? Banging my head to stop the noise. To stop the hurt. The hate and disgust I felt for myself were profound. I couldn't look at myself in the mirror. I wanted to make my face a piece of art.

There was a phase I wanted to wear how much I was hurting. I wanted to feel the pain outside, it felt far more manageable than what I was feeling inside. Dark purple hues stretched across my arms, my hips, blues, and sickly greenish greys across my cheekbones and thighs. I wanted to break. I'd punch so hard my fists hurt. I scratch and scream and make myself bleed. Lying breathlessly distracted and oddly relieved from the torture of being trapped in my head.

I can't tell you how hard that is to write, tears springing up as I linger in the memory. Fear starts whispering, "Now they'll know you're crazy, only a psycho acts that way."

I won't hide from my ugly side. I won't let my past haunt me anymore. I was dealing in the best way I knew how. It reminds me of a favorite writer. *"Only when we are brave enough to explore the darkness will we discover the infinite power of our light"* Brene Brown.

It's hard to look at our ugly sides and stare at them straight on, but when you do, they can't hold power over you. They thrive in secrecy and darkness, much like Vampires - they can't survive the light.

All I wanted then was for the hurt to stop, promises to stick, a happy family that played together and had fun. I wanted more moments like the weekends when we would be watching Saturday morning cartoons and keep ourselves entertained until we would hear the sounding cry of the summoning whistle that would get Charlie, our moody cocker spaniel, racing upstairs to get to dad first and we would trip over our feet trying to get there before him. Charlie always won.

My dad tells me afterward that they came to London to see me in ICU - a large dialysis needle stuffed in my main artery of my leg to filter my blood and keep my kidneys from failing, a lifeline in my chest, and hooked up to monitors and IVs. I was unconscious for 6 days in critical condition. I was in and out of consciousness for the week that followed after that.

Every time I came to, my body ached, I was exhausted, my head was in a haze.

Everything hurt. Every movement was agony. I was restless and weak. Sometimes, I would remember what happened. Other times, I'd ask to go home forgetting where I was and how I had gotten there. My head was constantly pounding and, when I managed to get out of bed, the room would spin violently making walking next to impossible. For weeks, food was difficult to eat. Anything that hit my stomach was revolting, turned sour, and burned the back of my throat, causing me to wretch or endure a stabbing sensation in my abdomen.

What I remember most from that time is Sean, a heavyset man, glasses always rolling down his stout nose. We were buddies in the ward. We'd tease and laugh during movies. He was one of the Child and Youth workers there. I remember stepping out of the taxi I took from the hospital that treated me, back to the ward I was trapped in "getting help". Going from therapy-to-therapy sessions, group sessions, medication after medication. I was feeling even more trapped, being stuck in here to protect myself from myself.

I wasn't expecting him to be joyful in seeing me. I didn't expect him to be mean. Then again, I didn't know what to expect. I was just struggling with the physical aftermath. He was so cold and abrupt. It stung. He lectured me on the long haul to the ward. Maybe I had gotten him in trouble. Maybe it was just easier to be angry. Maybe he thought he'd get through to me to never do something so stupid again. I don't remember any of what he said. I just remember that he was so angry and disappointed with me. I'll never know.

> *"People will forget what you said, people will forget what you did, but people will never forget how you made them feel."*
> — Maya Angelou

This brilliant plan came from a Simpsons episode, a show I watched religiously. The family is visiting France and Bart comes across the scandal of the company putting antifreeze in the wine. No one will know because it is sweet and tastes like alcohol. Bart saved The Parisians from being poisoned. I was so close. I was that close… that…close…to succeeding.

Raised Catholic and having been protected far too many times in my life to have kept up a count over the years, I believe, as Abuelita did, in Angels. We always prayed before bedtime and asked the Angels to watch over us.

My angels guided me out of that hole where I could have easily curled up and never awakened. There on the cold cement, with $2.63 left in my pocket. Just enough for a slice of pizza.

My angels couldn't stop me but they exposed me. It wasn't my time. Whispering to me "The stream, you have to get to the stream." I remember hearing it in my delirium. Was the police officer looking for me? Or did he see someone inebriated heading right out into the busy flow of traffic? Though I have lost faith in the corruption and politics of organized religion, I do feel a presence, call it the universe, God, a greater power. My soul was not meant to go home that day, despite my desperation.

As I pour into tears, remembering this story and my body reliving the sensations of escaping and the rush of adrenaline, I could hardly keep my fingers on the right keys. Memories I have kept long-hidden and forgotten flash, again and again, re-feeling the harassment and wish. Remembering how powerless I felt to stop feeling that way. The wish that things were different and that I didn't feel this was my only choice.

My alarm goes off and pulls me out of my past. It's time to get the boys up for school. I go upstairs to wake my beautiful boys and stifle more tears and the realization of the miracle I had been given hits me all at once. A mom of 4, married to my soulmate, the only sense of home and belonging I've ever felt since those dark days. I could have missed all this.

My heart fills with gratitude for what could have been erased – a life full of love and laughter, memories and learning. I would have missed their sweet embrace or the way they light up when I see them after school. I would have missed laughing so hard with my husband playing card games by candlelight that chocolate milk threatened to shoot out from my nose. I could have missed meeting my mother-in-law and experiencing some of the most loving and sentimental embraces. I would have missed seeing my mother heal and find her joy and power again, blossoming into the person I only saw glimpses of in childhood. I would have missed our heart to hearts. I would have missed my wedding, my speeches, my first videos, when my son got into bee boxing, or my daughter and her love and unbridled enthusiasm of snails and snakes. I would have missed running a home daycare with families I adored and children I loved. My daughter taking her three brothers out for a drive. I would have missed hiking with my best friend, having a few too many drinks, and testing my flying skills off the dresser onto the bed. I would have missed it all – publishing my first book... and the many things I have yet to do, speaking at sold-out events, people wearing my art, traveling the world and experiencing a whole other way of life, and the many memories and milestones yet to come. There is much more life to live.

My dear reader wherever you are in your pain and your journey, keep going. There is a whole other world past this pain. There are memories to make, people to meet, wounds to heal. There are milestones for you to discover, and power deep within you to embrace.

You are still here and you have a choice.

What if the lights just stayed out? What would you miss?

What if…

Trust the process. You are still here.

People don't remember what you say,

they remember how you made them feel.

- Maya Angelou

LIFE IS A
MYSTERY
EVERYONE
MUST STAND
ALONE
I HEAR YOU
CALL MY
NAME AND IT
FEELS LIKE
HOME

- MADONNA

Chapter 12 – I Hear You Call My Name...

I look out of the frosted windows from the second floor coming back from a bathroom break at work, out to the sea of snow-covered cars in the parking lot. A heavy sigh escapes. I think of the snow that will inevitability get in my boots and up my sleeves. Back at my computer, three times in a row I've had to double and triple check the numbers I'm entering in the computer, details for the next order.

My brother's getting married this year. I find myself battling feelings of attending or not. We had it out a few months ago over differences of opinion. He lashed out, digging up my insecurities and guilt, allowing them to sit exposed, putrid and rotting. The stench stung my eyes. I told myself I'd never speak to him again.

If it was just him, there wouldn't be such a conflict in my mind but I adore my soon to be sister-in-law. A joyful and energized soul, with an endearing French accent, and charm that wedged deep in my heart.

The hurt parts of me still asking, "Why him? What does she see in him?"

The radio on the dusty cabinet top comes alive, notes float through the air and carry the haunting call "Life... is....... A........ mys.... ter,.....y." A memory rises and I'm transported as I see my 4-year-old self-rocking out to Madonna. I see my dad, sitting on the edge of the bed, the soft glow of the side lamp and the echo of my voice giving the performance of my life to my beloved Papa.

"Hello, Leee, yaaaa, anyone there?" my co-worker interrupts my daydream

I snapped back.

"You, ok??" she asks

"Yeah," I beamed at her. Half of me was still lost in the memory. "Do you know this song?" I asked.

"For sure! I always love me some Madonna." She starts to sway and rock to the beat.

"I haven't heard that song in years. I remember begging my dad to let me perform one of my dances before bedtime. I finally wore him down and I know I got at least three more songs out of him after that." I tell her in a blur.

"Awe that's so sweet!" She smiles.

"When you're done with this, we need to work on the next file." She gets back to work and hands me another box to go through.

"Sounds good," I reply and get back to work, almost forgetting the moment as quickly as it had arrived.

Wrapped up in the cocoon of my sheets, the house is still. The hum of the pellet stove, which normally lulls me to sleep, keeps me company in the darkness. Wide-eyed, all I see are the memories as they flash through my mind, holding tight to my dreams, demanding the ransom of my undivided attention.

Lost in nostalgia, I hear laughter, feel the connection and bond of small moments, an all-encompassing hug that keeps me warm though winter slides through the cracks of our 19th century home. I can almost smell his aftershave. The charcoal of his hair is littered with fine strands of silver. I see his whole face light up in a smile. I smile at the way his shoulders shake as he chuckles at my shuffles and spins.

The fortress of my heart had been burst open and I was not prepared for the tsunami of emotion that followed, bright, fierce, and in full color. It had been years since I had thought about my dad that way. To my joy and horror, I was reliving some of my happiest memories. I found myself on a rollercoaster without brakes, trying to slow down and only gaining speed.

Anger surged to the surface interrupting my joy, then suddenly drops into the bowels of sorrow, making my heart throb, only to be lifted back up into another happy memory.

Long family bike rides through the rolling countryside, flying down valleys then having to turn around and haul me and my bike back up the hill, dad calling from behind, "Keep pedaling! Keep going! Don't stop!" The moment I'd hit the top without having to dismount and walk the rest of the way up, everything was said in the look we shared.

Or those times when we went "window shopping" in the mall, music playing to entertain and add to the shopper's experience. My mom's face drained as my dad picked up his air guitar and started to dance through the stores. Stopping to shimmy and shake on the spot. My brother and I laughed and danced along taking full advantage of dad's carefree joy, watching as mom slid out of view.

Stifling laughs, I remembered Saturday morning rolled-up newspaper fights. Dad, along with his 9-5 sales job, also delivered newspapers six days a week before we got up to get ready for school. We always had extra newspapers lying around. Now and then, we'd chase each other and try and land a whack without allowing one to land on us - running wild, sucking air between nervous giggles.

Whack! Whack! Whack. Whack. WHACK!

We'd join teams, then turn on one another, Whack, whack…

Newspaper pieces flying everywhere, call for a truce, breathing hard trying not to choke on our laugher.

I remembered, mischievously satisfied, at how easy it was to sway him into a treat or hamburgers for lunch. All we had to do was let out the trademark "aye-yi-yi" and pull out the big puppy dog eyes. When we got older, we'd set up the adorable youngest brother to turn on his charm to get us all the goods. Dad would always smile and look almost apologetically at my mom and shrug as if he just couldn't help it. "The kids want to."

Or the memory of sitting in our parents' bedroom, while Dad was trying to find a shirt for his job interview the following day. He pulls up one sleeve then the next. He has a pair of pants already on but unbuttoned to allow him to tuck in his shirt. He then tries to button the pants and the look of absolute horror that crawls upon his face is one that I conjure up when I need a laugh.

He sucks air in hard and fast making a "eeeehhhhh" sound, looking at us, his pants, then back at us. His hands rubbed over his belly. "eeehhhhhh – What's this? Impossible!"

He looks in the mirror "eeehhhhhh."

He looks at my mom.

"You need to stop putting my clothes in the dryer! Do you see this?!?"

Mom rolls her eyes.

Yeah, she's seen it and made it very clear every second helping, desserts, or the dutiful tax he's taken from us kids at meal times. He looks back at us, the pants, "No! No! NO! eeehhhhhh," looking back at the mirror.

He adjusts his pants again as if they have gotten caught up on his hip at an odd angle, and he will find the extra few inches he needs to close the gap with a quick adjustment. Then vowing to start his diet and exercise regime on Monday, complete with garbage bag gym sweats to maximize full sweat capacity. He lasts 15 minutes on the stationary bike before he was showered in sweat.

As these happy memories flash, I snap back hard, as if walking towards the bright sunshine and warmth only to have the door slammed hard on your face.

Hot fiery anger followed, why? Why, was this coming up at all? I had buried this and gotten over this already. Memories of everything he had done to our family growing up flashed again and again through my mind, mom crying, belts, hiding, the stalking Dread, screams.

The anger built as I remembered his need to run mom down to justify his actions and try and get me on "his" side. The way he twisted whatever happened. He never kicked me out, "You left". Yet he drove me an hour away asked me if I had any money. Then, when I said "no", he LEFT, without another word. He had no idea where I'd go because I didn't even know.

My stomach turned as I remembered he just up and left the country and walked away from us all, especially my younger siblings who were 9, 2, and 1.

He maxed out credit cards in both their names leaving her with over 30k in debt. If that wasn't enough, he took the stove after she asked if her and the boys could please keep it, they needed it. He took it anyway and sold it for money he used to fund his departure. I felt nauseated. I was there.

My face burned as I remembered the last time I saw him. Then, cracking through was a wash of a fresh ocean wave flooding in to cool the anger and bring with it the longing I had been ignoring, stuffed deep where I couldn't see or feel it, trying to set it alight with my fury.

As I write this, my 6-year-old is just starting back to school again after being home for the past 18 months of the pandemic. This morning he woke up angry and crying, everything bothered him.

The light was too bright, the breakfast was too cold, the orange juice too sour. The socks were too tight and the sweater was not right. Getting him out the door was a challenge. It took me a long time to understand that when we feel bad, we act bad. I sat with him and just held him until the storm passed enough to get ready without more drama. His little body was tight and rigid slowly melting enough to get out to that bus.

Later that night, after stories and a cuddle he told me that at school he was really sad and he was trying to hide his sad face.

"Why were you sad?" I asked.

"I missed you, I just wanted to come home. I was making me mad so they didn't see my sad face."

Ohhh…That's why the morning was so rough.

My 6-year-old stirred a question in me. Why is it we protect ourselves with anger?

Anger gives us strength to battle, to keep face, and fuels our drive to conquer the enemy. Sadness leaves us exposed, vulnerable, and hurt. Anger is active and makes us feel in control and powerful.

Sadness is passive making us feel helpless and ashamed, something even in our early years we feel we need to hide. This is the sadness I was trying to hide. The longing a daughter feels for her dad, a moment, even if it's an imagined moment when you felt safe and protected.

Over the next week, I felt like a pendulum swinging from anger to sadness. My whole world, everything I believed, everything I valued, just didn't make sense. I found myself questioning everything. My heart ached for that dad I knew as a little girl, the glimpses of moments when he was who he wanted to be, a family man.

I thought of the last time I saw him. I thought of the anger I had when he tried to bring up the past. I thought of the emptiness I felt when I came home. I thought of all the empty promises, the years that were between us. I thought of all the memories I wouldn't have. My brothers. My home so many years ago. My mom. I thought of my jerk brother who was just a mirror image of the man I grew up with.

Then as soon as that thought crashed through, I was hit with wave upon wave of emotion of what it could have been. I saw the life we would have enjoyed if he had stayed, if he had been the dad, we needed him to be.

Sadness, for not having my dad in my life all these years. Him not being at my wedding though, to be fair, I didn't invite him. My children do not have a grandfather to meet, play with, and spoil them. No sitting at the dinner table and sharing stories of our childhood. No warm hugs, no visits, nothing but silence.

I'd remember times he pushed me to keep trying in sports and rollerblading though I was hopelessly uncoordinated. The way he completely renovated my room and invested in tile floors, air purifiers, and therapy, for my severe asthma. The countless hours he worked to provide for us and spoil us with experiences, trips, and toys. I cried because I believe that once upon a time, he did truly love me, love us.

Yanked back into the anger of everything he wasn't and everything he was. How could someone be so kind and generous yet turn and be so cruel and heartless? If I had a relationship with him, I would be saying that everything that happened was ok. I was somehow "letting him off the hook" and justifying what he did.

This isn't happening I can't do this, "No! No! Stop. I am not willing to get hurt again. It's been 15 years since I talked to him. It's impossible. No." I stuff down not only the happy memories but the dreadful longing.

It didn't matter where I went, reminders always followed me. Always showing me what I was missing in my life. At weddings. Visiting friends. School events. Holidays. Movies. The pain showed up as anger, irritation, surges of jealousy, and bitterness followed by the questions.

Why not me? Why was I not worth staying for? What happened to unconditional love? What's wrong with me? Why do they get their family? What did I do?

When these feelings came up, I had convinced myself that I didn't need him. Anytime the longing of a little girl who missed her Papa bubbled up, and the possibility of "maybe we can", I reminded myself of everything he had done, all the ways he hurt us, all the destruction and pain he caused.

I never really stopped to consider maybe he was hurting too. Stubborn, I convinced myself I was better off, I could do this life thing better. I was going to do it "the right way". Then life came by and pulled me back into reality. Job loss, postpartum depression, a marriage hanging on its last threads, loss of a surrogate parent after watching her slowly fade away into dimentia and your only family and support living a day's drive away in another province.

I struggled with the idea that I wanted anything to do with him at all. I tried to deny how I felt and tried to ignore the feelings that were bubbling up inside me, telling myself it will pass. Remember everything. You haven't needed him this far. You don't need him. He's only going to hurt you again.

There comes a point when you can no longer continue to battle, your resources are depleted, the emotional toll leaves you exhausted, you are cried out, your rage has reduced to a low simmer. You aren't even sure what you are fighting for. A war within can never be forever. Sometimes the war is not even something to be won.

What now? I couldn't go back to my fortress. It had been torn open, destroyed. I was exposed.

Looking in the mirror eyes red and swollen, dark circles, my face looked pale, pained, and drained of life. Looking at this sight I had to ask myself, "What is it you are so desperate to hold on to?"

DON'T CALL THE WORLD DIRTY BECAUSE YOU FORGOT TO CLEAN YOUR GLASSES-

ARON HILL

Part 2:

Clean your Glasses

Chapter 13 – Dirty Glasses

At 3 years old, I was playing in the nursery that was being built for my soon to be born baby brother. I've always been one of those kids who like to pick at things, glue, scabs, boogers, today the window sill glue had captured my attention. I was digging away at it with my fingers but I couldn't quite get the grip on the silicone. Flustered, but not enough to be deterred, I looked around the room. The shine of a discarded nail caught my eye. Perfect. Pointy. Small and narrow and bonus points for being shiny.

It sunk in easily into the warm silicone and I started scrapping and picking. I found it so fascinating how I could dig the nail right in under the white gooey substance and how it would stretch when I pulled to the right and then to the left. I started sliding that nail across and it got caught, so naturally, I pulled up. I was not going to let up.

I won against the silicone but lost against the nail. I sunk that nail right into my left eye. I yanked it out and ran to my room, clutching my weeping eye.

"Time for lunch" dad called. I kept my gaze down and away allowing my hair to fall in my face. As much as it hurt, I was more afraid of getting in trouble.

My attempts to hide my punctured eye didn't last. In a few short hours, I was in a weird-smelling room with a huge shining light and people surrounding me.

Someone told me, "Count back from 100." as they started to place the black mask over my nose and mouth.

"But I can't count to 100". I countered.

Laughter clattered together and I was instructed to just count backward from 10 then. Dutifully "I counted 10, 9, 8" … swoosh.

By some miracle, I managed to miss my lens by micro millimeters and retain my sight what I got, instead, was a lifetime of wearing glasses.

My dad always cleaned my glasses. When I got them back, they always felt cool, smelled of lemon, and made my world sparkle.

When the responsibility was passed off to me, I was too busy doing things. I never really got around to it. Now and then he'd grab my glasses and say, "Ligia, how can you possibly see out of these things?"

Why clean them? I could see alright. I never could tell the difference unless he pointed it out.

When I traded my clean lenses for the dirty, cracked lenses he wore, marred with a lifetime of trying to navigate his new world, my story and his made a different kind of sense. I was trying to hold on to this idea of how things should have been. According to what I wanted to see in my life, for my mom, my brothers, my family as a whole. What I thought "everyone else" was living.

I had to come to terms with the idea that this story wasn't one I had written but I had the choice to interpret my role as a victim or take some sort of action to relieve my pain. I had played the role of pained victim. It was a role that left me anxious, depressed, and spinning out of control in my life. I had come too far and worked too hard to go down that road, again. There had to be another way.

A quote popped up in my social feeds:

> "Empathy is about finding the echoes of another person in yourself."
>
> – Mohsin Hamid

And I found myself walking through what I imagined must have been my dad's experience.

Empathy can be a tricky subject for people. It was for me. I had this idea that, if I tried to understand my dad, I had to agree with his point of view. Somehow, I was giving something precious up – my values, or code of ethics. Somehow, if I considered thinking of him as anything but a monster who destroyed my family, I would lose that standard and it would infect the rest of my life. If I allowed him to "get away with it", what did it say about me?

When you have been hurt by someone's actions or lack of action it is very hard to even consider this because we tend to look at the experience from the point of view of "I could never do that." We interpret others' actions and experiences from OUR point of view and life experience. In the realm of our experience, it's unthinkable to behave in a way that could be so hurtful to another.

There had to be a "winner" in the view of the past. Was I operating from the standard of I am above these turns in life? I had to ask myself, "Have I lived my life in such a way that I can claim behaving perfectly at all times? Was I angelic in my temper? Did I always understand what people meant? Did I always communicate my needs? Have I never made terrible mistakes? Hell no!"

I learned how to be better because the people around me gave me grace and saw something better in me, allowing me space to learn and grow from my mistakes but setting boundaries to say "Hey, that's not ok." "If you need something, ask." "If you are angry, go for a walk, don't take it out on me." I learned to read books on the topic and expand my awareness and understanding of psychology and leadership. I was in an environment where it was safe to ask questions, be vulnerable and had access to resources.

What if you didn't have that voice of reason? What if those resources weren't available? What if you had the core belief you had to "man up" and handle your business?

What if, over time, things compounded at such a confounding rate you found yourself thinking, "Who the hell is this?" Not knowing how you got there in the first place, let alone figuring out a way back to you – the "you" you thought you were. Your thoughts and emotions so loud and consuming, having such a hold on you, you can't hear which voice is really yours.

There was enough evidence to convince me that maybe there was part of the story I was missing. I got curious and started asking myself a different set of questions:

What went wrong? Why did it hurt so much? What was it I wanted? What if I walked in his shoes, how would I see this?

Boiled down, I missed my dad. I missed that sense of home. I missed his ridiculousness, the way he'd give the steering wheel a shower when he sneezed. I wanted my kids to know him, the parts of him I carried with me, my roots and beginnings. My dad lived out loud in full color when he was living. I was old enough to catch glimpses of it between the storms.

I had to understand: Why did he give up? What happened? I had to believe in something bigger than my own point of view if I wanted to have any sort of relationship and come to terms with our shared past, not for fact gathering and blaming but to put the pain away once and for all. Was it even possible? I had to try.

I heard this story many years ago where I'm not even sure, but it has forever changed how I look at blame and I use it often when my children are in the throws of the blame game:

Imagine you are in a canoe paddling down the river with a friend. You're going along everything is great, until you notice the current getting stronger, bumpy and you are moving faster. You look far ahead and realize you are headed for a waterfall. Somewhere you've taken a wrong turn. Your canoe mate has given you the wrong instructions. Do you start yelling and blaming them for their mistake and get into an argument of whose fault it is, or do you work together and paddle like hell to get yourself to safety?

It illustrates to me how futile arguing is, how irrelevant and damaging blaming is. The only gain is to the ego which is an empty pursuit as it is, because the ego will never be satisfied.

To move on, I had to find a way to reconcile the two worlds – one of protection, standards, and ethics and the other of home and belonging.

What did I need to believe to make this union possible?

Another quote came to mind.

> "Empathy has no script.
> There is no right way or wrong way to do it.
> It's simply listening, holding space, withholding judgement, emotionally connecting, and communicating that incredibly healing message of 'You're not alone'"
>
> —Brene Brown

"Opinion is really the lowest
form of human knowledge.

It requires no accountability, no
understanding.

The highest form of knowledge
is empathy, for it
requires us to suspend
our egos and live in
another's world."

-Bill Bullard

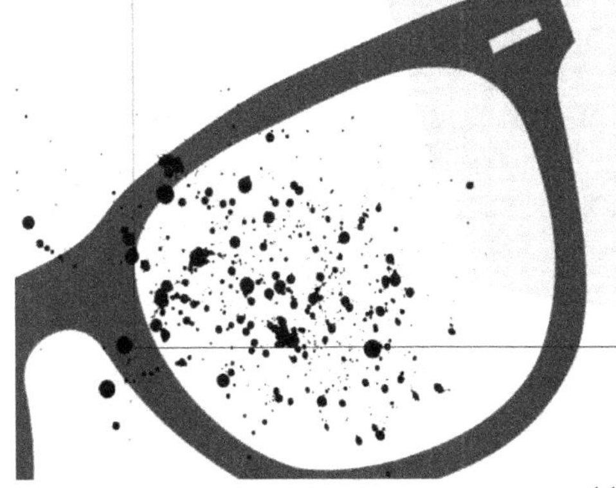

For the first time, I stepped back and put myself in my dad's position. I went back as far as my knowledge, memory and imagination could take me.

I had to imagine what it must have been like for him to pick up his young family and move to a new country, when you barely spoke English. To move to a country with snow and ice, when you are used to the year-long heat and sunshine. Driven to succeed and provide, starting in a feather mascot costume at minimum wage to creating a 30k a month cleaning business. All while battling what was later diagnosed as bipolar disorder. Let's add to that mix the standards of what it means to be a MAN, coming from a machismo culture. Who do you turn to when your world is falling apart?

What about his longings for home where the world made sense? Dealing with losing his mom to aggressive cancer shortly after his daughter was born. His older brother was captured, tortured, and killed fighting against the corrupt government. Missing his father, his siblings, nieces and nephews, cousins, and uncles. He went from a vibrant village to total isolation.

I think of my own life and how I have handled all the setbacks, disappointments, failures, and hardships. I had the advantage of being here, most of my life and being raised in Canadian culture. I had the advantage of education, being a native English speaker, being pale white like my mom to the point where most people who meet me don't believe my heritage is Spanish.

As I was writing out the history, it broke me out of my arrogant mind and fed me a mouth full of humility and respect for what it means to adult.

Does any of this excuse the time I sat crying in the corner of my principal's office bathroom at 7 years old because I was terrified of going home? Does any of this excuse the fact that the only out my mother saw was to down a bottle of pills to escape the tyranny? I've carried the scars of being belittled, told I'm too fat, useless, I'll never amount to anything... weighed regularly and put on rice cake diets. The intimidation, threats, objects being flung, the welts, the bruises. No.

No, it doesn't excuse any of it but I can move forward with compassion and come to a place where the story took a turn outside of his control and he lost his way so profoundly that he felt attacked at all angles and was just fighting to survive in the most basic way he knew how – like a cornered animal.

Hurt before you are hurt. He couldn't take the pressure from the outside much less the demons that tormented him inside. Every failure on the outside turned up the volume on the inside. He wasn't "enough." Every time we, as kids, carelessly broke something, didn't show appreciation for all his hard work, he took it as disrespect. We didn't appreciate all the sacrifice and hard work, the countless hours he put in. He was so out of control in his own life he turned to cultivate control in any way he could.

When I traded my clean lenses for the cracked and stained ones he wore, our story, our experience was not suffered alone. He was suffering too. We all were. So very alone, just trying to get through.

When we feel bad, we do bad. When we don't have the tools, we fix the problems in the only way we know how. We turn to premoral instincts to satisfy our basic needs.

A year or two earlier, my mom shared with me she wrote a letter to her dad, unloading all her feelings. The letter never made it to him but it was a cathartic experience for her and allowed her to finally leave the past where it lay. Nothing can be changed from the past. She decided to move forward and start over with her dad.

So, I wrote my dad a letter. My focus was to remember the good times, the memories that tugged at my heart. I thanked him for what he did do, he brought us to this country, away from a bullet found in my crib, from a civil war-torn country. I acknowledged how hard he worked and how alone he must have felt.

I thanked him. I invited him to start from this point forward. I was not interested in reliving the past. Nothing came from blame. He had his hurts. I had mine. We could start from here, and move forward.

It was not pretty or magical but he brought us here for a better life, for opportunities he will never enjoy. We have luxuries we take for granted as he finds ways to survive back home after giving us his best years and youth.

He sacrificed for us. He hurt us. He saved us and gave us the best life he could with the capacity he had.

There's a peace in knowing his intentions were good. When you are writing the story as you go along and forging your path with no one to light the way before you, is it not natural to take wrong turns, to keep going even when riddled with disease? We carry on in the only way we know how to. Life doesn't wait for us to figure it out. There's not pause button o restart.

I could look at my dad's life through his lens. I didn't need him to admit anything or acknowledge the past. I didn't need him to apologize. He still hasn't to this day, but it's ok. I don't need his apology.

He has his guilt, evidenced in the explaining, justifying, manipulating the events to his favor, twisting motives to fit with his story so he could calm the anxiety racing through his veins, haunting his dreams. I don't need to punish him. He has to live with himself.

It was the first time I understood what it meant to forgive. I wasn't letting him off the hook. I was letting myself go, from the hurt, from the pain I had carried for years. I could finally let it go and find peace. His story was not mine to judge and condemn.

> "Holding on to anger is like drinking poison and expecting the other person to die"
>
> -Buddha

I decided when I wrote that letter no matter the outcome, I had done my part. I was grateful for this revelation; it was a gift that gave me peace.

At the most basic level, I was reminded that we are all human. We share the same moon and stars that stretch out across the sky. We share the same chromosomes though all expressed very differently. We crawl before we walk, we cry before we talk. We have the same core basic needs, food, shelter, and love. We all laugh and cry. We all want a better life. We all want to be better than we are. What if we stop arguing with what was and accepted where we are without judgment but with an extension of love and appreciation at how far we have come? What if we extend that same grace to those, we want to love around us?

Exercise

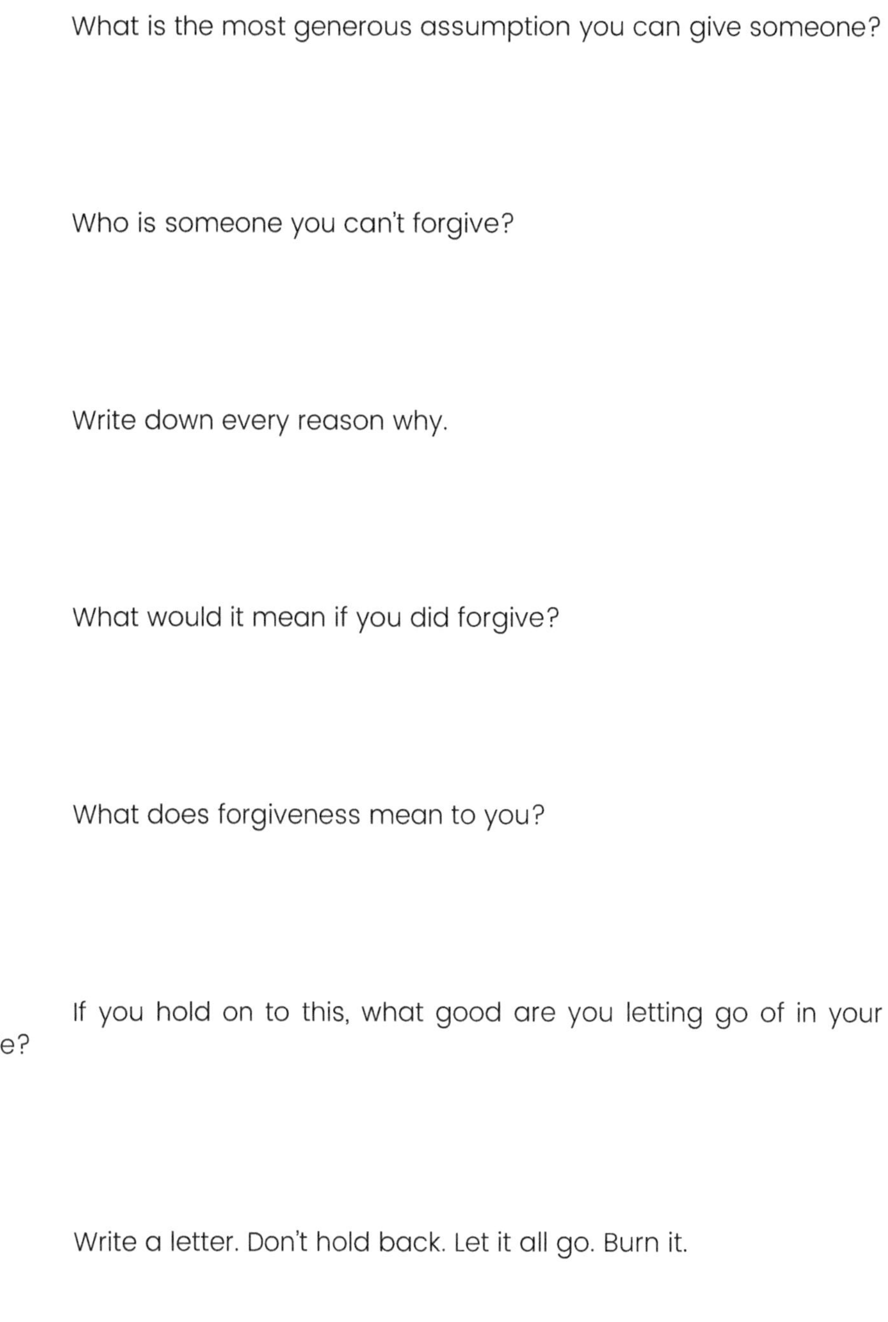

What is the most generous assumption you can give someone?

Who is someone you can't forgive?

Write down every reason why.

What would it mean if you did forgive?

What does forgiveness mean to you?

If you hold on to this, what good are you letting go of in your life?

Write a letter. Don't hold back. Let it all go. Burn it.

WHEN THEY DRESS YOU UP IN LIES AND YOU'RE LEFT NAKED WITH THE TRUTH

- PINK

The hardest thing in life is letting go of what you thought was real.

- Mareeze Reyes

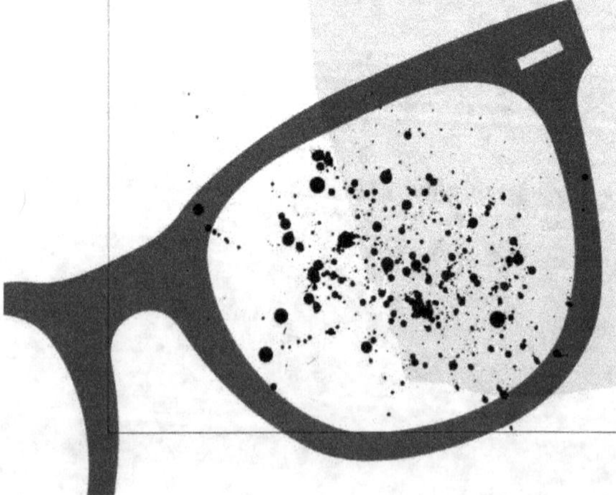

Chapter 14 – The Lie of Negativity

Where is it? Where did I put the soothers? Why can't I find anything? What time is it? ARRRHHHH I'm going to be late…. Why can't I get my sh%$ together! The rampage in my head as I riffle through drawers, frantically looking in cupboards, convinced I've forgotten something, yet again. I'm supposed to be leaving for Quebec in less than 2 hours, on a 7-hour bus ride. Abuelita is visiting and we are spending time together with my baby girl. Her first great granddaughter.

My phone rings interrupting my thoughts.

It's Abuelita. "How are you?" she asks.

I unload, in a rush my frustration and agitation, to try to be ready on time. Spewing out words faster than sentences can form. In the way only a grandma can:

"Ligia Elena, Stop. If you don't make this bus there will be another one tomorrow and you have more time to prepare, why are you getting all worked up?"

I feel like I've just been slapped in the face.

"Ok", I said. "I just want to see you. It's my first time taking the coach. I'm just worried if I forget something."

"If you do, your mom has things here." She soothes

"If it's too much stress stay home another day, I can't wait to see you when you get here - whenever that is. I'll let you go to pack" she ends with a kiss-kiss on the receiver.

I hang up and suddenly feel so silly for spinning out that way.

I have a choice.

I can make this experience miserable and stressful not only for myself but those around me and those who will have to deal with me when I have worked myself into such a state of hysterics. I will no doubt lash out at some unsuspecting person. Or, I can take a minute to breathe, write down what I need, and just pack it. As long as I have the baby, a few clothes, and myself, that is good enough. Make a list, lay it out on the bed, anything to make the stress pass, this is supposed to be an enjoyable experience.

One of the hardest things, in coming to terms with our pain, is realizing we have a hand in creating the misery we are experiencing. It's a hard pill to swallow - to realize that we are creating our sense of dis-ease and stress by how we are approaching a situation. It's hard because we believe it should be a certain way.

We have an expectation of how things are supposed to go - based on what? Based on our past experiences, our imagination of a best outcome that we decided would be the scenario that makes us feel in control, make us feel safe, picked up from what we witness in our culture, what we consume from the media and our everyday interactions and culture.

Why are we spinning out? What if we met every moment with a sense of curiosity rather than expectancy of how things are supposed to be? With curiosity, you ask questions and seek to understand, informing the way that you respond. With expectancy, you have a set scenario already in your mind, and when that scenario isn't going according to plan it feels like an attack on your being, which causes you to react to the bubbling of emotions as a result.

We don't always have a choice with what happens to us, a lost job, a car accident, illness, when a loved one passes on, a breakup, there are so many times in our lives when things are happening that are not fair. We didn't deserve that treatment. We didn't see it coming. We have 100% choice in how we look at the challenges of any situation and how we choose to move forward.

One of my favorite sayings is:

> "I am convinced that life is 10% what happens to me and 90% of how I react to it. And so it's with you... we are in charge of our Attitudes."
> — Charles R.

How can I look at this in a way that makes me feel empowered instead of discouraging myself and my efforts? I have found when I look at things from the perspective of progress, I feel encouraged and want to continue to look forward and continue to put in the effort. When I am looking at every way that I am lacking and how I am not where I think I "should be", it's discouraging and lowers my overall energy.

Can you imagine if you could put a microphone inside your head? What would the conversation sound like? Would it be things you say to your dearest friend? Would you say it to someone you truly cared about? Probably not.

We are wired for negativity, to always be on the lookout, it's what has pushed us to survive this long. Up until now, this is an evolutionary function of the primal brain to ensure our survival. With our rapidly changing world, our brains have not caught up to our ever-changing needs, our lack of imminent danger and the abundance. We are experiencing our brains are still on the lookout for any and all threats. That's its main function: keeping us alive.

Maybe like me, you were wired from a young age to learn to survive one crisis after another, trying to clean up before the next one, leaving you always on the lookout for any subtle hints and warning signs of when it's coming. The shift in expression, the energy in the air, the tone of voice...

With practice and self-awareness, you can learn to recognize and catch those thoughts before they lead you down a road of self-sabotage and self-destruction. Maybe it's eating that donut you vowed to not touch to help you reach your goal weight. Maybe it's blowing up at your kids for not cleaning their room. Maybe it's the way you read that e-mail that got your heart racing in anticipation of a needed defensive response.

There are times when you are in the moment and see yourself and wonder why you are doing this, but the momentum is already too far forward to stop it. We can stop it. We can take a breath and slow it down. If you are near water, splash your face with cold water. Changing your physiology will change your state and slow the spiral down, slow the charging freight train from causing unintended damage.

A little story to illustrate: My daughter has struggled with food intolerances since she was little. We only discovered this because her moods would shift from joyful to dark, angry, and reactive.

When she ate wheat, she dealt with severe stomach aches, pounding headaches, and an overall feeling of fatigue would consume her body. No wonder she was so moody. How do you react when you are fighting a cold, are in pain, and fighting with fatigue, aches and pains? Maybe you could get by without reacting for a day or two. When it's the constant state of your life and you just ache to feel what you think is normal, you are in a state of fight or flight to get out of pain. I know I am comparing physical pain to emotional pain but stay with me. I have found the outward reactions are the same.

When I am consumed with feelings of inadequacy, or not feeling that I am enough, feeling guilt, re-living a poor choice I made again and again, I am so lost in my head. Then someone starts prodding me from the outside. I don't feel good, so I don't do good. I lash out. I get a surge of emotions that bubbles up. I feel defensive and ready to attack. Anything that might threaten the story I am playing out inside gets the reaction. When we are stuck in worry and pain, when we are consumed by negative feelings, it's hard to come out of that place and respond with grace.

Things That Helped Me

Take time to acknowledge, I am not feeling right in my body, and be ok with that. Stop judging how you feel. Stop thinking you "should feel" a different way. Stop fighting it and sit with that feeling. Allow yourself to feel. All you have is this very moment. Accept what you are feeling this at this moment but love that you are.

WHAT?? Are you nuts? How can I LOVE feeling down, anxious, depressed (insert crappy feeling here)???? That's the last thing I want to do!

Our bodies are amazing, intuitive organisms that are constantly giving us information. We often ignore it, trying to deny or outright fight it. Your feelings are trying to get you to look at something, bring something to your awareness. Emotions are the messenger. Look at it as of you got some mail.

I tell those around me I am not feeling quite right. Take time to determine the source of the discomfort. Did I get enough sleep? What was my diet like today? When did this start? Did I drink enough water?

Move. Make a change in your environment. Do an exercise routine. My favorite is to write it out, let it all flow, don't hold back. I can literally see what is trudging around in there and reframe it to what I actually believe. I'll never forget writing down stream of consciousness and literally rereading what I wrote and thinking, "that's not even true, I don't believe that at all". We get into trouble when we believe that all the thought trains up there are valid and worthy of our attention. Try paying attention to the thoughts that empower you.

Try one. Try many. Do something out of your routine. Do what feels right to you.

Our reactions to the outside world start with us. Though there are circumstances and people who trigger us, how we react has far more to do with what is going on with our inner worlds than our outer world. We mirror our experience and add meaning to what is happening based on our past experiences. All we have is this very moment, this very breath. Take a deliberate breath. Make a choice and decide how you want to respond in this situation instead of reacting to your outer world and experience. The only thing you have absolute control over is you. Don't give away your power. Stand tall within it.

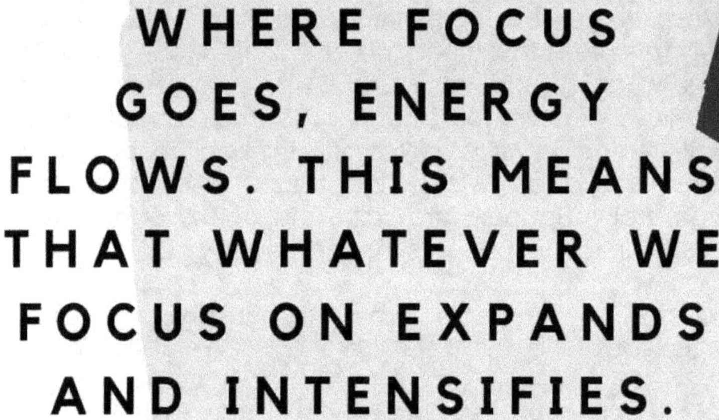
WHERE FOCUS
GOES, ENERGY
FLOWS. THIS MEANS
THAT WHATEVER WE
FOCUS ON EXPANDS
AND INTENSIFIES.

-TONY ROBBINS

Chapter 15 – The Lie of Realistic

I've often been drawn to comedians - the way they engage a crowd and tell a story. They extrapolate the everyday aspects of all our lives and show us a whole different angle, one that shocks and entertains. One who has come into my radar more recently is comic, Kyle Cease. He shared a story about being realistic that really helped me shift the way I was looking at my creativity and how I think about reality.

He said that we have this habit of looking at reality through the lens of the negative, we measure our future based on what we already know from our past. What we forget to do is realize that there is always an opposite side, what we will gain. What if we stopped focusing on the potential pain and loss and started putting the emphasis on possibilities, opportunities and potential for improvements? Which motivates you more?

Our culture leads us to identify our negative aspects and work harder on them to eradicate them and get better. Often, we are working so hard against ourselves we are left frustrated and feeling even worse.

What if, instead, we focused on our assets? What if we come out improved and on top because we feel supported? This is not to say that you should stop working on the areas of weakness. My suggestion is to focus more on where you are strong and can make more impact.

Had it not been for trying to improve my "weakness" in communication and public speaking, I would not have discovered my passion for performance, spinning stories, and connecting with an audience. In this case, focusing on my skills to improve had to do with how I saw myself. I had a clear view of the person I wanted to be. One of my biggest hang-ups was that I could barely make eye contact, let alone speak to anyone without wanting to run into the bathroom to hide. I was lacking in confidence and had crushing social anxiety. Yet, I felt deep down there was a part of me that had a voice, a personality that was buried within the fear and rejection of my past. What do you, deep down, whisper to you?

Why do we insist on arguing for our limitations? Why do we argue with what is?

> "If you argue for your limitations, you get to keep them. But if you argue for your possibilities you get to create them"
>
> — Kelly Lee Phillips.

Exercise

Feel the differences in these phrases. Which leaves you feeling empowered? One is helpless, limited and cut off. The other offers possibility for improvement and faith.

- I'll never get a job. vs. I am getting closer to the job that is right for me.
- I'm terrible at writing. vs. Every day I practice and I improve a little more.
- I can't do this. vs. I am learning more about how to do this every time I try.
- There is no solution to this. vs. There is a solution, I have not found it, yet.

Yet is a powerful little word that gives space for possibility and encouragement that is on its way to becoming reality. We have this idea that reality is based in the negative. Reality can equally be effective and positive. Reality is what we choose to see. Reality is the meaning we attach to an experience.

Why not work with yourself? Why not make it easier on yourself? You can find success that can be far more joyous and enjoyable when you aren't focusing on everything you are lacking. What have you done? How much have you progressed already? How can you get excited about this? You don't need to see the whole staircase but if you know the direction you are going in, you are getting closer to where you want and can take the next step.

Patience is key. Life is a marathon; we often try to sprint through not seeing that we have a choice to realize that, no matter what we want to do, it's never too late if we start in the direction of that goal now.

A note about self-talk.

The language in our minds happens as automatically as breathing. Much of the way you talk to yourself and process your world is based on programs installed in your early years and throughout your development. One thing to understand is most of those programs were not put there by you. They are the ideas, thoughts, attitudes of the people and culture and the environment you were surrounded by. They all influence the way you think and interpret your world. We don't even realize the things we are saying to ourselves. We take what's in our minds as truth and don't often stop to question what is being said. We may want to change how we think but we often revert to our patterns and automatic responses. Our brains seek out comfort and familiarity.

Things that worked for me:

I wrote down the type of person I wanted to be in the present time language. A full page of the best version of ME. Not who anyone else wanted or expected me to be but who wanted to be.

- I am a …
- I enjoy…
- I am excited to…
- I (am this) …
- I get to…

I kept this piece of paper folded up and, in my pocket, and read it again and again throughout the day. Right after waking up, after breakfast, in the afternoon, and, especially, before bed. When I was alone, I read this piece of paper aloud, with energy and conviction, proclaiming that this is who I am. I recorded it on my phone and listened to it during a drive, doing the dishes, any free moments during the day.

I did this every day for at least a month, eventually, I didn't need to take the paper out. As I read through the paper, I'd imagine what that version of me would look like, how she would stand, how she would dress, how she would interact and be present.

If this sounds crazy to you, that's ok, but I ask you, isn't it crazier to constantly be putting yourself down and thinking poorly of yourself? Isn't it crazier to wonder why you can't do what you say you are going to do? It has taken a lifetime of you thinking in this limiting way that has created the programs and habits running through your mind. It is so automatic you don't even realize its happening. If you want a different life, you need to be a different person and to be a different person starts with your beliefs. If it still sounds crazy, let me ask – Is what you are currently doing driving you to stick to goals and show up in the way you want to?

Those automatic systems had hi-jacked my brain so profoundly, that I despised myself and tried to destroy myself and my chance at life. The thing was, I had no idea what was happening. I had no idea I had a choice. You truly start believing this. This is it. This is what you've got.

You have a choice. I challenge you to write down some of the garbage you say to yourself daily. Don't stop there. I challenge you to write its opposite and practice that belief. Give yourself a break. What is the most generous assumption you can give yourself? Write down 50 amazing things you have already done in your life. Remind yourself of who you really are.

Break the cycle: This is the easiest and most relatable example I can think of:

I'm fat vs. I am losing weight. I eat healthy all day.

Let me ask you – if you think you can't do something and you are going to fail would you be open to trying again? Do you tell yourself, "What's the point?" If you do, are you going to keep showing up?

I recently started a passion project: a YouTube channel ("To check it out scan the QR code or search leahspeltligia on YouTube") It's a place to share stories and create fun effects and emotions with video. This project has opened a light within me that makes it impossible to ignore. I love writing the stories, piecing together the video, finding the perfect song to convey the feeling. I love reviewing it again and again to make sure I have the right effect. My husband often laughs at me and my big goofy grin while I'm in the process. I can't help it. I'm in the act of creating and it brings me so much joy. Despite how happy it makes me my ego can get in the way, old stories and insecurities start bubbling up and I start questioning what I'm doing. THIS IS OUR AUTOMATIC STATE – especially when we are doing something new, when we are tired, hungry or dehydrated.

I cannot stress the importance of reading, listening to and surrounding yourself with positive media. What goes in comes out. Garbage in = Garbage out. Consuming negativity (i.e., news) will leave you to feel depressed and down, helpless and conscious.

Listen to biographies, stories of triumph, people who have come through challenging times and how they handled the problem. What was their thought process? What motivated them? What did they have to believe to get through the difficult times? There is so much history before us that someone, somewhere can be a beacon to relate to. Our specific set of experiences is unique and there is no one size fits all but there are clues everywhere. Since I have had this habit for so long, I hear the negativity descending on me but feel and hear the wisdom I have carried rise up to challenge those automatic thoughts and keep me on the path.

Write it down. Write down your negative thought and challenge it. Notice how it feels in your body. Rewrite it. Remember there is always a better feeling choice. Be your own best friend.

When we feel bad about ourselves and look at all the places we are lacking, we shy away from challenges. We have deficient energy. Over a prolonged time, these negative ideas manifest themselves into habits that sabotage your efforts.

When I experience depression, I see that I am living in opposition to my truest and most vibrant self. I've convinced myself I have to be a certain way. It is the hardest, most exhausting, damaging thing we do to ourselves. It takes extraordinary effort to work against who you know is true and deep down inside of you. Sometimes it takes getting to a pain point to make you say "I don't want to be this person anymore" where we can fall apart and rebuild.

Looking back, I see the times when what I had worked so hard to get to fell apart. I didn't realize it at the time but this break down was creating space to rebuild something new. When I let go of the attachment to what it was "supposed" to look like, I allowed the process to inform me and made me open to other opportunities.

It gave me space to reframe past experiences.

Trust: Start building trust within yourself. This starts by picking up a pen and being open and raw about what is floating through your head. Read empowering books. Learn about what happens in our heads. Surround yourself with people striving to improve themselves too. Do what you say you will do. Keep promises to yourself.

What three things are you grateful for? Gratitude is powerful but not for the scope of this book. What I will share, though, is when you get into this habit you start noticing all the things you are grateful for, your three will easily become a list of ten. You'll start seeing your blessings everywhere.

When you are being particularly hard on yourself, think about how a friend would look at you. Put on your friend's glasses to look at your life and your progress. How would they see you? What would they say? What would you say to encourage yourself as a friend?

One more thing: Whenever life is throwing a difficult time at me, a situation that disrupts everything and turns life upside down, I **catastrophize** and think how could this be worse and count my blessing up from there.

A few years ago, I had a terrifying experience on a slippery Canadian winter road. I was with my three children and we spun out across the highway. Shaken and scared, we finally came to a stop on the shoulder facing on-coming traffic and my vehicle had lost all power. I imagined spinning out and being hit by on-coming traffic, I imagined we hit the foot of the bridge, that we fell into the ditch, we stopped in the middle of the road. With thinking of all the things that didn't happen I was able to stay focused and grateful in the moment, accepting our situation for what it was.

What are the absolute worst-case scenarios? Then, what?

ALL WE
HAVE
IS NOW

Chapter 16 – Follow the Weird Wonderous Calling Song in Your Heart

"In This Game, Fire Represents Your Life" –Jeff Probst

Our favorite show, one we watched as a family, was Survivor Night with Jeff Probst. We'd talk about who was the next to go, hold back gags when crushed tarantula soup was choked down, or feel the ache as the survivor slipped, smoking his arm, on a pole as he fell to the ground.

We had snacks during these tv times, but not the ordinary Canadian ones I've come to know. Dad's favorite was radishes sliced thin with onions, salt, pepper, and vinegar, we loved a firm green, just about to ripen, sliced mango with a sprinkle of salt, giving the best combination of tart and salt that makes my mouth water. One of my favorite treats was invented by my mom. She'd pop a pot of popcorn on the stove, with oil and salt, heap it in a big bowl, then grab a cup and spoon from the counter. I sat beside her as she scooped away at her snack. I dove into the fresh popcorn. The smell of pickles tickled my nose.

"You're eating pickles! Can I have one?"

"I don't have any." She smiled.

I look at her hands, just a cup, a spoon and some sort of liquid in the cup I assumed was tea or juice.

"But I smell it!" I accused.

"It's my snack," she says as she drops a handful of popcorn into her cup and scoops the soggy, pickle juice-soaked popcorn into her mouth.

I am half grossed out and half curious. Curiosity wins and I run to the kitchen for a cup and spoon to try out this concoction for myself.

It's weird but oddly satisfying. Every time I look at pickles or popcorn it always makes me think of my mom.

I learned from my mom to experiment and take chances on what could be - to be bold and take chances with opposing, new ideas, to question what "normal" is. Though people might look at you funny, you might also inspire curiosity and have someone join in and try it out too.

Our lives don't follow a typical path. There is no instruction book or grade system to reach for. Yet, somehow, we reach a point where we look around and think to ourselves "I should be further ahead than this." You find yourself dressed in embarrassment, the stains of shame, of not measuring up. Looking at all the ways "they" had every opportunity. "They" had a life I could only dream of. "They" didn't have to go through this. "They" had this or that.

I used to get so caught up in that story that I started to feel like I was living my life all wrong. I had lost the script. I was messing up my lines. I was in the wrong movie. When I became a parent for the first time, I read every book I could think of, some ideas conflicting with others. The list of best practices mounted and I just never felt like I could do enough. A seasoned mother told me "Do what feels right for you. You know your baby best". You know yourself best.

I realized that I could write my ending. That just because the beginning started with doubt, heartache, and trauma didn't mean I had to continue to carry the residue of that pain with me for the rest of my days.

I used to feel like a wide-eyed child near a shop window, salivating as they put the delectable chocolate truffle cake right in the display window. A thick plane of glass between me and my hopes and dreams. Something I could only see and wish for.

Don't ever think that showing up and challenging that narrative is easy. Don't ever think that just because you see smiles and confidence means it's easy. It's hard. Worthwhile things ARE hard to do.

Being fit takes effort. Showing up for what you believe in with zero proof that it will amount to anything takes courage. It means that your dreams have to hold more value in your psyche than your fears of what you are going to look like to others. It means accepting that resistance means you are on the right track. It doesn't mean you aren't ready. It means you are pushing past what comes easy and are growing. It's uncomfortable.

It is scary but the only way out of the pain is through it. You have to be a little braver. Embrace the adage "Whatever - let's do it. Why not?" attitude. It's normal to feel the resistance every day. That nagging little voice that tells you that what you are doing doesn't matter. That you are a joke. That people think what your doing is dumb. That you are wasting your time. Don't you have better things to do? How selfish.

What would happen if you welcome the dream-sucking vampires in? Pull up a chair and serve them tea and invite them to chat. Listen. Acknowledge. Then, thank them for their concern. Say you'll consider what they say and wish them a good day. Then, go do what is in your heart to do.

When you fight these demons, you give them power. They feed off that attention. You give them your most precious resources - time and energy.

It's ok to be afraid of something new. You've held those pains for so long that the thought of letting go makes you feel naked and vulnerable. It feels like you open yourself up to looking stupid, being misunderstood, abandoned, or being hurt, again.

Ask yourself - what would life look like if you weren't afraid? What would you do? How would you show up? The stories in our minds are powerful. We need to get to a point where you are more afraid of getting to your death bed and feeling like you never lived. We are more than animals whose main instinct is to survive. We were equipped to thrive.

To this point, we feel the energy all around us, the tension of a room, the energy when someone talks about something exciting, the calm of a painting.

Trust those vibes.

When is it you feel most alive? What are you doing that makes time fly? What makes you almost feel silly for loving? This is your magic. Get curious. Explore it. Practice it a little more. Since when do your doubts get more merit than your dreams. Those nagging little whispers of ideas and desires came to you. See where they lead you.

One of the most important habits I have adapted is trigger words. When I am feeling stuck, lacking energy, downright grumpy, I think back to pickles, pickles, and popcorn It reminds me that it's time to experiment and stretch. It reminds me that I'm thinking too small, too black and white.

What can you try out today?

Scan to get your workbook or check out the YouTube channel and stay connected

"AND THE DAY
CAME WHEN THE
RISK TO REMAIN
TIGHT IN A BUD
WAS MORE
PAINFUL THAN THE
RISK IT TOOK TO
BLOSSOM."
— ANAIS NIN

Chapter 17 – These Clothes Don't Fit Anymore

Sometimes there will be rough patches, you'll feel like you have passed the worst of these negative feelings then, suddenly, you find yourself in a place that feels heavy - as if someone dumped a pile of sticky tar all over you but you have enough clear space to suck a few deep breaths before the tar engulfs you.

If not for four children depending on me, getting up to face the day felt like torture. It was like trying to walk when you have been sitting in a cross-legged position for far too long and your legs have lost the blood flow needed to allow for muscle function.

All the best advice says exercise, eat well, get enough sleep. Check, check and check. It's been my life, but lately, exercise made the anxiety worse. Usually, when I run my mind produces some of my best ideas. My body is busy, so my mind gets creative to distract and entertain me. During this season, I'd sooner find myself in a heap on the floor sobbing, I felt I would suffocate on my tears, all instigated by free-running thoughts that didn't serve me.

I tried to carry on, as usual, to hide it the best I could. I put on the brave face, I was strong for my family until my resolve, my strength, the thick armor I protect myself with started to crack.

Bang! Each time I came up short and I couldn't get a handle on my boys. Crack! When I couldn't understand my preteen. Slap! Boys fighting. Crunch! Every time I couldn't connect with my husband broke me a little more.

It went on like this for a few months, it was always there but easily pushed back down, except this time it wasn't going down, it wasn't receding no matter how I tried, no matter how I fed myself with positive reinforcement. I was drowning and didn't know how to make it stop. I felt trapped in a room and my only hope was dishing out spoons full of water at a time. An illusion at best, those spoons full had nowhere to go. Where was this water coming from? Why couldn't I stop it? A better question still, how did I get into this room without an exit? No window? No door? Trapped.

I got to the point and backed away from the point of believing I needed therapy. I needed to talk to someone. It took another month of fighting myself to take the plunge. Then I cried when the woman I had finally chosen asked me why I wanted to come to see her. I saw her the following week.

My heart bled that session. Waterfalls of tears and pain flowed freely and seemingly unstoppable until mid-cry she let me know we had five minutes left and I had to pull myself together. I mopped up my sloppy tear-showered face and got the hell out of there as fast as I could.

Then a few days later I wrote her a letter:

Dear Maggie,

Thank you very much for your time and meeting with me but I will not be needing your services.

After our first session, I left there completely and utterly naked. It was as if the nightmare of my childhood dreams had come to life. I was stark naked and in public. I am a modest and private person by nature and the level of exposure and vulnerability I left with that day made me need to run and hide.

The rest of my day was rough. My little boys were acting up, it seemed as if I was pulled in every direction and it was a grind just to get to the point I could just sit and breathe again and piece together what had happened and where to go next. I felt especially sensitive, quick to anger and insufferably down.

My best friend asked me how our meeting went and instinctively I told her I didn't think it was what I needed. I shared with her the main insights I drew from the experience and my confusion as to where to go next.

Seeing my husband later that evening he asked me how our meeting went. After having some space and time to think about it I realized how much past hurts had affected me and shook my trust.

It was such an uncomfortable conversation, painful, heavy, and slow. It got to the point I just couldn't do it anymore. Sitting there in silence unsure what to say. Feeling the words strangled at my throat, but I still had so much I had left unsaid. I couldn't carry this anymore.

I cracked open what was left open of a month-old bottle of my favorite full-bodied red Cabernet Sauvignon and let the cool dark burgundy moisture hit the back of my mouth, so hot with holding on too tight, holding back words, feelings, and unspeakable hurts.

It felt like steam as the wine flowed, calming, softening edges, unwinding the spring of my body that was far too tight.
Into my second glass, it got real and I came to terms with 3 main ideas:

1. I am only a failure as a mother if I quit trying, which is not in my nature. Stoically stubborn is more my way.

2. When people left me, I didn't die. No matter what happened I found my path and kept forging on building my life, screwing up, and trying again. My life does not depend on anyone. If my husband dies, if my longtime family friends leave, if my real family leaves... if everyone left I would not be alone, I will not die without them.

3. I am still me and I will always find a way. I always have.

I shared with him how much it meant to me to live on purpose, how I feel I need to find my purpose.

Patience and appreciation for where I currently am were lacking in my equation. I forgot to appreciate myself and how far I have already come. I was only looking at what I was not and how I felt I was failing.

I felt the haziness lift and literally like a switch the next morning I knew it was over, and I felt myself again.

I have been down this road before and understand what it looks like. I recognize the patterns. What I didn't realize was how I got pulled into it, how it had taken over so completely, why I didn't stop it sooner.

No offense but I am so done with this path, therapy, and looking at what's wrong with my life. I feel like it just brings me back to a broken version of whom I used to be and takes me backward in my journey. My family depends on me to move forward. My future self depends on me to keep moving forward.

I also realized I cannot squander the gifts I have because of fear of vulnerability, being judged and exposed. That would hurt far more than any abandonment I could face because it would be the abandonment of myself.

It feels as though I opened a long-forgotten door to my past and tried on a few of my old clothes and forgot how to do up the buttons and zippers. I realized these clothes no longer belong to me, they don't fit anymore, they just aren't my style.

My vision got clouded, my heart felt, broken but in my studies, I have learned to make sense and live with my madness. Embrace it and make it work for me instead of against me.

Thank you for allowing me the space to leave it all on the table and walk away completely exposed so I could find the clothes that fit me best.

Sincerely Ligia

Please note: I am not suggesting in any way that therapy is not essential for healing. I am an advocate for doing what works for you. I had been in some form of therapy for 6 years. Therapy was likely helpful since it made me become more self-aware and recognize the stories, I had been telling myself. Therapists are people who ask me questions I hadn't considered and challenge my way of thinking. It's all the years of therapy, study, and writing that got me to the point I could source out the root of my distress.

I was feeling left out, left behind as families grew and expanded, life changed, routines shifted. I no longer fit into the lives of the people who were there for me and welcomed me and my family, as their own when, I had no one. We had drifted apart. I got an invite to a wedding but was not included in the preparation and planning. I was heartbroken. Once family, now just a guest.

I was feeling abandoned again. It brought with it the theme of my life of being abandoned by the people I loved, who I believed loved me and would always be there - my mom, my dad, friends, even my grandma. It made me question why am I not worth sticking by? Why am I so different? Why doesn't anyone like me? Look at me failing. No wonder. No one wants a loser.

It was another area of life where I felt helpless. I felt isolated and lacking community, friends, but in this season, I had to learn to be my own best friend and promise never to abandon myself. I anchored in that realization that I had no control over what happened around me, people come and go, act badly, hurt you, die, betray you. What do we have when it's all taken away?

Just you. That's all you need to start again.

These people in your life are a gift, a present of a lesson that you are meant to learn. They give you examples, some a dark page of what you don't want, to help you understand what you do want, what you need.

The relationship you have with yourself is vital. No one owes you anything. I don't care if they brought you into this world, if they promised to be with you until the bitter end, if you had the best times together. Each moment and interaction is a gift, one to be appreciated, cherished, and released. Take the lesson. Build yourself.

What clothes are you wearing that just don't fit anymore?

What are the themes that keep coming up for you?

What is making you so sad?

What is true about who you are?

Have you been through a hard season?

What worked for you back then?

What does the best version of you think?

What does the strongest part of you think?

If this is a stretch, what does your best friend think about you?

"Life isn't about waiting for the storm to pass, it's about learning how to dance in the rain."
– Author Unknown
RESILIENT

Chapter 18 – Quit Hiding

It was on a crisp fall morning as the dew still shone on the grass, the damp leaves dulled the sound of my footsteps like a blanket under my feet. I was walking back towards the barn to lock up. My eyes traveled up the edge of the stark white painted door and there, right on the layers of paint in various stages of peeling, I saw something strange.

We all have our place, our purpose. It's sometimes small and subtle. Other times, it's big and world-changing.

Now and then, the hidden creatures that are created to blend into their surroundings want to explore a different and new world that makes them stand out and seem out of place, more vulnerable to predators. Yet on the other hand, how can we appreciate their unique qualities if they are always in hiding?

During this time, I was fascinated by all the beauty held in the little things around me. The veins in leaves, The delicate striations under mushroom caps. The way frost kissed berries show the outline of every intricate edge and depression. The shadow of a leaf upon another leaf in just the right light.

The things we so easily bypass without a second thought. I was drawn into a micro aspect of life. I felt like I had stepped into a whole new world of beauty and a world of wonder and got thinking to myself why don't we see this? Why am I noticing this now?

I always wanted to hide, to be invisible. If I stepped out and dared to be seen, I was muzzled and put neatly or brutally back in my place. I carried these lessons throughout my life.

Protected by the walls of my home for the past 16 years, I felt like I was in a bubble. I had no idea who I was, no idea what I could do, and if anyone would even care. I felt like I was still always hiding.

Always playing the chameleon. At home, in friendships, out in public. Always afraid.

On a crisp fall day, I was helping a friend with farm chores. Feed the chickens, collect the eggs, milk the goats, catch the goat that ran away. Goats are fussy eaters. They need fresh hay every day.

I saw something that didn't belong. It was a dark long shape about the size of my hand. I had never really seen one outside before. There on the door, was a cigar-brown stick bug.

I was struck more by the fact it was not camouflaged. These creatures are designed by nature to blend in, to go unnoticed, to disappear among the branches. Yet here was this stick bug in all its sticky glory - knobby knees, endlessly long antennas, its long angular body, just hanging there in plain view.

I imagined the tiny claws he must have on the ends of his limbs that allow him to be able to stay in that vertical position. It stood there in stark contrast to the weathered white paint of the barn door. I couldn't help but stop to watch him. What was he doing out here? He could be picked up by a bird. I could squash him. A rodent might find him tasty.

I felt a strange interest in this bug. They can be still for hours. They can change colors to blend in. They can regrow a limb if one gets yanked off.

But what was he doing against a white painted door???

No grass. No branches. No place to hide.

The idea of this stick bug, just out in the open, weighed on my mind throughout the day. Did he get lost? Was he confused? What was he thinking? He was so far from where he belonged, it didn't make sense.

But then maybe I was being too closed in my thinking.

Maybe he was tired of blending in and being invisible. Maybe he needed to change things up and try something new. Maybe he wanted to be seen, by someone, anyone.

Maybe I needed to see him that day, to understand that just because I may have been molded to play small, to hide, and to be invisible to survive doesn't mean I have to live a stick bug life. I could stand out in my way. Yes, there are risks. Yes, not everyone will like you. Yes, well-meaning people will want to put you back in your place. Today you can decide to take on the courage of that stick bug, to make your difference, however small.

I believe lessons come in all forms and I believe if we are open enough, we can learn from even the humblest of creatures. The world is working for you if you are open to seeing it, if you can slow down enough to hear it. Heed its lesson and have the courage to do something you have never done.

How can you possibly know who you are when you are always in hiding?

How can you possibly know what you are capable of if you are always trying to blend in with everyone else?

I still think of that stick bug, saying come brave little creature, come out to play, and explore this scary new world with me.

Take some time to go for a walk-in nature. Put your phone on airplane mode. Take some time and really look at the miraculous world around you. Take some time to look at things close up. Appreciate what it would take to replicate such a scene. There is so much we take for granted.

What are you hiding from? What would happen if you came out to play? What is it costing you to stay hidden?

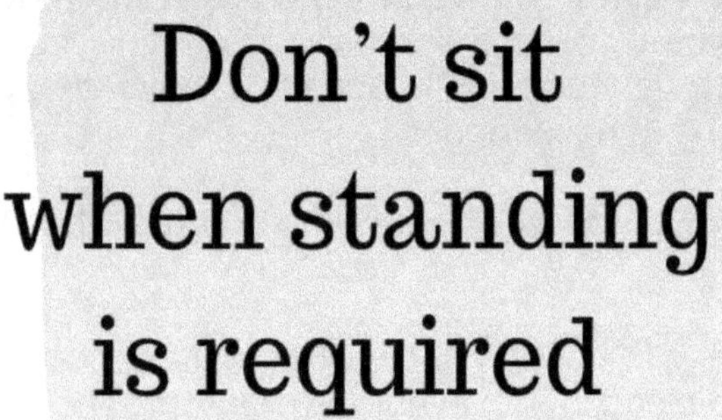

Don't sit when standing is required

-Shane Koyczan

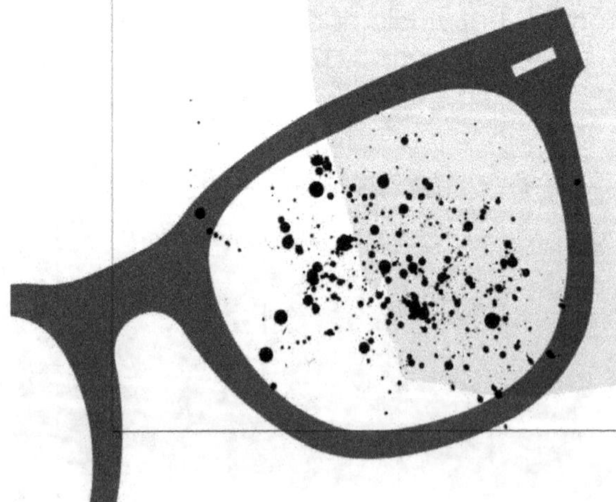

Chapter 19 – I Wish I Could Have Told You

Dear past me:

Today I met with a health coach and friend. We talked about all the hurtful patterns we get trapped in – the things we turn to, or behaviors we engage in, all to protect ourselves and help us survive our experience.

We mirrored in our mission. One pain reflected in another. A call to move us into action to be the light of the crusade and forge the path. Saying, I know of the relentless dragons and treachery within these trails. Let me be your guide. Let me show you the way to safety. It is my pleasure to give years back to lives, years that we lost learning and growing in the struggle.

I think of all the challenges you have faced in your life. The hardships, the broken hearts and body, at times plagued with an illness that stopped you dead in your tracks, the broken home, but ultimately, by far the worst was working through your broken self.

I can't help but look at you and wish I could have taken all the hurt away by letting you know there was a cure, a method to stop the madness, relief for your ache. I wish I could have shown you the power you already had.

I wish I could tell you the right things to say – that you were worth standing up for, that you had a voice. You were allowed to use it, you needed to.

I wish, I could have been there to hold your hand and help you to understand that what you were doing was hurtful, what you were doing was so unnecessary. The ways that you were trying to drown out the pain, to numb it, to silence it, all of it, was only hurting you more.

Every time you pushed people away, you did more damage and left yourself a little more alone. One day you would get so good at it, so good at avoiding people and situations, making elaborate excuses, that you would look up and see there was no one left to run away from. All you have left is you.

I wish I could have told you that the desperation of wanting to fill the void was anxiety and that no matter what you put into your body to try and push it out, it would only make you feel worse. There is a better way.

I wish I could have told you that the pain wouldn't last forever and that like a storm it will pass. Like the seasons, things will change. Some storms will be more violent and raging, leaving an aftermath of repair and clean-up to do. Figuring out where these pieces all came from will feel impossible. But you'll figure it out.

I wish I could have told you that you are everything you will ever need. You are enough. You are worthy. It's important to learn to be ok with you.

I wish I could go back and tell you that you are more than your sickness. You are more than your pain. More than all the excuses. When you were struggling to push down tears after being left out in the cold, I wish I could have shown you the future.

I wish I could have told you, just be honest, stop lying and fabricating these elaborate stories to try and fit in, to try and explain yourself away, to try and find love and acceptance. It only pushes people away. People aren't stupid. They know. They always know.

I wish I could have told you that it's OK to want things. It's OK to put yourself first. You can be of service AND take care of your needs.

I wish I could have told you it was OK, it is ESSENTIAL to dream, to hope, to wish. Your visions are of value. It was OK to look stupid. It was OK to mess up. There is no shame in not being perfect or not naturally gifted. It's safe to take up space. It's OK to learn and be a work in progress and own that, 100%.

If you knew that, you would have picked up that pencil sooner, maybe you would have held on to that paintbrush. Maybe you would have finished that book in your heart. Maybe you would have danced.

I wish I could have told you, no, scratch that, SCREAMED AT YOU… STOP MAKING IT SO FREAKING COMPLICATED AND QUIT WITH THE EXCUSES AND JUST START ALREADY!!!

Then, again, we all bloom in our own time.

Just start doing the thing you want to do. The thing your heart keeps calling you to do. Stop judging it, stop saying it's so impractical. Listen and try.

But then, I think you wouldn't be who you are today if you knew all along the right things to do. You wouldn't understand how to navigate through pain and struggle. You would be completely inept in this ever-changing world. If I had told you everything you need to know, it would have been too easy. You would be spoiled, entitled and always expect life to be that way.

I would have stolen from you, your deep appreciation and gratitude, stripped away your joy and enthusiasm for life, your compassion and sensitivity to others, empathy. You would never know what that is if you weren't so misunderstood yourself.

I know as you go through your journey, one of embracing the successes and leaning into the difficulties, people will come to you and show you how amazing and easy it has been for them or the people they know. It will feel almost like they are mocking your efforts. You will be tempted to look at their lives and say well they didn't have to go through this, and they had that going for them.

Don't. Don't do it. You have to know that although we don't always show it, we aren't always aware of it, we don't always want to admit it, we all struggle. We all have our stories.

Don't let it phase you. You are on your journey. You can take pride in your process and own who you are. You don't need to be afraid.

Just keep going.

All my love and appreciation,

Ligia Elena

Exercise

Write a letter to your past self.

You are more than your pain

asking for help isn't weakness

You always have a choice

it's ok to cry

Life is happening for you

Confidence is a skill

You are stronger than you know

You are exactly where you need to be

You are not alone

Follow your curiosities

You do enough, you are enough, you have nothing to prove

You are more than your pain

Lessons are repeated until learned

Without Struggle

THERE CAN BE NO

PROGRESS

Chapter 20 – Finding My Voice and Community

Locked in the bathroom stall not daring to move for fear of setting off the motion sensors that would trigger the light, thereby giving away my presence in the bathroom stall, I held my breath. Not daring to breathe when someone came in to use the restroom. Praying my boots would hold up as I stood on the toilet, hands pushing against the walls of my miniature bunker.

As the lights go out after the last person has washed and dried their hands, I am left there in the darkness with aching muscles and thoughts.

"What's wrong with you?" "What on earth are you doing here?" I scolded myself for my absurd behavior. "You're acting as if someone is out to murder you. What is this?" Stuck somewhere between my terrified self that felt this was the only rational option to take when confronted by having to talk to people you don't know and not having the distraction of little children to run off with. Part of me knew I was far more capable than this.

I had run a busy, always full, childcare service out of my home for over ten years. I could talk to anyone. I was an active member of the community, networking, meeting other caregivers and new families. Who the hell was this? Hiding in the bathroom stall waiting for the time it was to leave.

It was one of the first times I had taken my oldest to hockey practice and their dad stayed home to put the other kids to bed.

Guilt washed over me as I was missing my daughter's practice but I didn't want to leave. My stomach was in knots. All because I didn't want to talk to the other moms? How absurd.

"What's wrong with you?", I admonished myself again. "Get it together! What kind of example are you being to your kids?"

I bullied myself out of that stall. I clutched myself tight and told myself to breathe. I realized something had to change. I had to do something about this. This wasn't me or any way to live. Something was still missing. I felt ashamed. Trying to gather up some sanity and self-worth. As I looked around all I saw was how I was failing. Why were these cycles still coming up?

Playing homemaker and child care provider, my whole goal was to make our home an extension of the family, a welcoming, educational fun environment where kids loved to come and parents feel good about going to work. 10 years I played the perfect mom and wife, I ran a business and kept the house clean and in order because I had to. I had a reputation to keep and I wanted to continue to attract new families. I was never without clients.

I did my job, I went to school part-time, made nutritious, made-from-scratch meals. I played that role. I never in my life experienced such a demoralizing loss of self as when I stopped bringing in my paycheck. I had always been working at something since I was kicked out of my home. Ever since I was I young kid, I worked in the family cleaning business. This was new territory. My family was everything to me. I wanted my children to have a stable home, with loving parents, and experiences of connection - to always feel safe and heard.

Instead of working, I would buy things on sale, I sold things we didn't need. I tried to do anything we could to save money and did the grunt work jobs around the house, digging up sidewalks, tear-outs for the renos. I did what I could to "earn my keep" and not leave more to the zombie who was my husband who was already putting in countless hours to support our goal of me being home to raise our two youngest children.

When the youngest came speeding into our lives (literally he was born in the ambulance we met on the way to the hospital. He just couldn't wait), all the color of my world drained.

I recognized the feeling. I had been there before. The numbness, heart-crushing hollow of feeling everything yet nothing all at once. The sensation of wanting to crawl right out of my skin. The constant feeling of dread, that I was somehow failing my children. No matter what I did, I could never do enough.

The screaming current that flowed through my body in constant alarm was an assault on my mind and sense of self. Drowning in the guilt for not being the person I knew I was. Dread anchored in my chest, making every breath and movement almost impossible. Forcing myself to smile and coo, and hold my babies and play with them because I knew this wasn't me. I knew this would pass. The memories of my first-born whispered reminders of hope that felt so distant and the path treacherous, yet it was there, it was possible. The guilt and shame you feel for even experiencing anything like this, is heavy. You know having a baby is a gift. You know friends who have struggled to have a baby, who have lost a child, and who have lost hope for a family. Here you are, blessed beyond what you deserve, and you are numb.

You look into that beautiful innocent face so full of promise and life. A piece cracks off your heart because all you feel is nothing. You berate yourself for feeling that way.

I fought to keep it to myself. I was a mom of four now. I had no time for this. I had no one to turn to anyway for the support of the other children. My family lived hours away and had their own struggles. My husband was working round the clock, his family distant and disconnected. Parents were elderly and needed support. I had no time for this. I was isolated, alone, with two small children, no family support, and nothing to look forward to at the "end of maternity". I was so grateful for my children, make no mistake, but the numbness and detachment that is a symptom of depression filters your life through a very harrowing lens.

I just wanted to stay locked up where I felt safe and away from prying eyes, eyes that would only judge, that would never understand. I didn't want to talk to anyone. I felt so shy and shifty when I did. I told half-truths to avoid explaining anything. I was always looking around when in conversation, always appearing just on the brink of having to take off after a child - anything to get me out of the interaction. I craved connection so desperately but I was so scared to open myself up to it and be vulnerable.

I went to community groups. I tried to engage and meet new moms but my nonverbal 3-year-old child would often be so overwhelmed with the environment he'd fall to pieces in a screaming fit. When the boys were both a little bigger, I wouldn't dare go anywhere even just for a short trip without my stroller because every time I did, I was usually stopped by a child who would lose their urge to walk and decide it was time for a tantrum on the floor. I was exhausted. Not only were the day's torture but they never consistently slept at night. I would often find myself sleeping on the floor or on a chair with them to keep them quiet so my husband could get some much-needed sleep before he faced the day ahead.

I was trying so hard to keep it together. My older kids were not adjusting well to the move we had made a few years before. They struggled to fit in and make friends. We went from being the place all the kids hung out in a busy city, to being out in the country and being surrounded by nothing but fields.

Serendipity came in the form of a Facebook post of an acquaintance sharing her win in a speech competition. My eyes widened and I was taken over by curiosity. What was Toastmasters? Speeches? I bombarded that person with questions and found a club near me.

Maybe this was my solution. Maybe this was the answer. Recounting this story to a group, the facilitator asked who goes to public speaking when they are at their lowest? I'd think therapy would be the thing you'd turn to."

I went as a guest for two meetings and witnessed a speaker who shared a vivid and entertaining story about work boots. I was captivated. Something in my heart cracked open. I knew then I wanted to do that. I was so excited. I wanted to join.

Life kept me as a guest who wouldn't return for two years.

In the meantime, I found a place to grow from the comfort of my home, to still be connected and available for my aging in-laws and my young family. It came in the form of long, luscious lashes. Scrolling through mom groups, lonely and disconnected. I had no job to get back to after "mat leave", my income had disappeared and I was looking for other options, not only for money but for a project. It started as selling make up for a MLM company. I was posting on my socials, making cute little mock-up pictures and videos of must-have products and funny ideas were always flooding my space. I could hardly sleep.

I felt a part of me come alive again, the creative, fun, outgoing side, that had gotten lost somewhere in between the move, rough pregnancies, and adjusting to country life.

It was never about the makeup though. I still found it itchy on my skin, dried my lips out, smeared and just felt unnatural on my sensitive skin. It was the community I loved. Women working towards a common goal, sharing ideas, helping one another, having fun, and liking and sharing posts. The environment of growing into a bolder and more capable version of you. One that wasn't afraid, one that spoke up, one that talked about the personal development books and inspiring people they followed. I loved the confidence and risk-taking it inspired in me. I was coming out of my shell more and more. I will always be grateful for that experience. It was a flicker of faith.

Moving away from the city meant accessibility was hard but essential in my journey. I relied too much on the familiar. I gave away my power constantly. My preference was to please and impress everyone else. In this space, away from the world I learned who I was, away from the noise, the expectation, the automatic life I was living.

My children grew a little more, my in-laws were in a better place, and I went back to Toastmasters. I signed up after my second meeting and I did my first speech by my third meeting. I wasn't about to waste any time this time around. I already experienced the pull of life taking me in the opposite direction. I didn't want to miss this opportunity.

I practiced and practiced, recorded and listened to my recorded practice. Being prepared will lower your anxiety, right? I was shaking like a leaf.

As scared as I was, I had come to a point in my life that I was just so tired of being scared. I asked myself what would life look like if I didn't let my fear stop me? Fear is always going to be there but what if I let it stay, and move forward anyway. What kind of example was I being to my children?

I knew something inside me wanted more. That I was capable of more but I kept stopping at the sweaty-palms, the desert dry mouth, the hive of bees in my stomach, the racing in my arms and shoulders. What if I did it anyway? I knew what to expect if I did nothing, if I stayed where I felt safe.

I started asking myself, what do I want to be proud of tomorrow? In a year? In 10 years?

I knew it would only feel harder the more I waited. I knew I would keep playing small. I knew I would keep avoiding situations that made me feel uncomfortable, making my world smaller and smaller… safer and safer.

NOOOOO! I promised myself if I was afraid that was exactly what I had to do. I had to be comfortable being uncomfortable.

I wanted more. I wanted to share the stories bubbling up inside me. I wanted to listen and learn from others' stories. I wanted to feel free.

The more I made myself show up and put myself out there, the more I was learning about myself, I was finding healing in the threads of my stories.

I learned the concept of courage creates confidence; confidence creates more courage. The more I showed up, the more I wanted to share the message, the more I wanted to be part of the solution. Joining the executive team pushed me to continually show up on days I didn't feel like it, when anxiety was getting the better of me and life just felt like it was a little too much. The commitment kept me going, if not for any other reason than I said I would. I was always grateful I did after.

Action steps

Find a community that speaks to you.

Get involved in something that means something to you.

Push yourself to do things that scare you.

Just start. Keep showing up. What scares you?

Why aren't you doing it? What would happen if you did?

What will it cost you if you don't do anything?

Be more scared of who I'll be, if you don't try.

"Start before you're Ready." https://youtu.be/L3wx9ki4SII

"Labels can
only CONFINE,
aspire to be
undefinable

-Colin Right

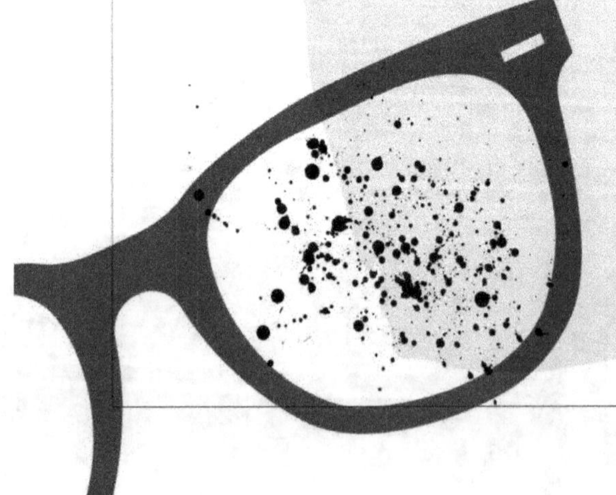

Chapter 21 – You Are Not Your Label

Do you like meeting new people?

Do you like helping people out?

What do you do if you have been unjustly blamed for something you didn't do? How long does it take you to calm down when you've been angry? Are you easily disappointed?

At our house, we had a gorgeous bookshelf we stained and built together as a family. It was filled with books. It was stocked with National Geographic magazines and brand-new leather-bound sets of encyclopedias: adult version and children's version. My parents invested in our opportunities to be readers.

As accessible and interesting as encyclopedias were, as early as 9 years old I loved nabbing my aunt's teen magazines. Looking at the dresses, learning about teen life and makeup was so fascinating.

After seeing the latest clothing trends and the newest hairdo, I'd skip straight to the tests. What kind of date are you? Hot or not? Anything that would give me insights into the kind of person I was. Nothing was more satisfying than counting up my tally. Then I would read my results, only to read another option and skew my answers to get that result - the result I thought made me look the coolest.

When is the last time you took a personality test? What's your avatar? What traits are more likely in you? Are you the mediator, the aggressor, the blah blah blah?

Though these tests can be fun to take for entertainment, they are hugely limited for learning who you are. Why? Because, you are deciding who you are moment to moment. What the tests capture is the decision you take most often or are most likely to take based on past experiences.

Take enough of these tests and you'll start to see patterns, little clues to tailor your responses and pick the answers that were close enough to what you might do in the given situation to be the person who you want to see yourself as being.

I imagined I would be a cool, fun, and popular teenager. That's the person I wanted to be.

As I took more tests, in magazines, books, mainstream tests, I found myself more and more saying well that depends, on my mood, time of the month, how things are going in life. Am I with someone? What's my health like? Have I moved recently? What's the vibe in the room?

Just before writing this chapter, I took another personality test. My results were predictable. What's interesting is that, if I had taken that same test three years ago, the answers would have been very different.

But why? If this is who I am, why are the results always changing?

The short answer: we get to decide.

Three years ago, I found myself hiding in a bathroom stall just to avoid a parent interaction at my kid's hockey game. Seriously. Assertive, powerful, and leadership were not in my vocabulary. Six years before playing a stand on the toilet and hoping your foot doesn't slip in, so you can hide from people role, I was confident, actively networking, and meeting people in the community. I called people who had gotten me clients in the past to let them know space was coming up available. I was constantly exploring different ways to connect. How did I get so shy? How did I get out of that?

After being in and out of hospitals and psychiatrist's offices and therapists of all sorts, I was diagnosed with a laundry list of labels to explain away my symptoms and constant state of suffering. These included but were not limited to, post-traumatic stress disorder, ADHD, dissociative disorder, deep depression, anxiety, and panic disorder. I was put on a cocktail of medications to treat the labels.

What kind of world would it have been if, instead of experimenting with prescribed chemicals, I had known I had a choice? What if people had asked me what did I see for my future instead of reliving the painful past? What if they had asked me what I would do if I didn't have to hide anymore? What if they had taught me the power of my mind and the effect of language on that system?

Words are powerful. These deficiencies and disorders, these labels, were given to me by panels of professionals judging me at various moments in time. Their only goal was to figure out what was wrong with me – how I was limited and flawed. It put me in a neat category and validated my sense of worthlessness and gave them a course of action.

My personality has evolved as a result of imagining the person I wanted to be, figuring out the skills the people I respected and admired had, and practicing them again and again until they became my identity. Understand these steps aren't rigid but can be seen as fluid markers of progress. Maybe they spell out your tendencies, help you be more aware of those tendencies, and work towards changing them IF that's what you want.

Our brains are designed to look for like things. Think of when you got a new car, say a red Dodge Durango. It's not a car you have ever really noticed before. You take it out for a test drive and on your way back home you start noticing Dodge Durango's everywhere.

A few months ago, a childhood friend posted about the missed signs of ADHD in girls. I commented playfully yup, yup and yup to everything. With smiley faces and shrugs. I was surprised by the comments that followed "I was just diagnosed, it's been hard", "my daughter has been diagnosed…hard, depressing, stressful, limiting" I was amazed at all the negative labels associated with ADHD.

I shared with them personally how much I have learned about these labels and how constrictive they can be.

The sense I got was they were trying to live "normally" – to fit into a stereotype of what they should be. They were living in a constant battle, because "it should be different."

How demoralizing and disabling. You catch yourself in the frustrating loop of not measuring up, judging yourself, and wishing it were different.

Labels - I have left all my labels behind and don't suffer from any of them anymore. I'll admit, I identify with them from time to time, all the hilarious ADHD memes, anxiety videos, mental health TikTok's because they are things, I see myself doing daily. My neck is stiff with the nods and fist pumps hollering yes, Yes! YASSS! If anything, these videos have given me a much better understanding of WHY I do what I do and learned to laugh at myself. I can ACCEPT that I was blessed with a different type of brain, embrace it and focus on building the skills and natural abilities I do have - those that don't come naturally to others. I credit my drive and creativity to this so called "deficiency". By learning how the mind of a person who identifies with ADHD works, I have also learned how to interpret and help two of my four kids who I see with the same tendencies, gifts, and challenges.

I hold strong that these labels, no matter what they are, don't have to be to the definition of you as a person. They are a part of you, not the whole of you.

No, we didn't fit in at school. We fell behind. We were punished and left out. It's not you. Systems were not set up to support our unique talents and abilities.

When I was diagnosed, at the time there were a lot of negative associations and ideas of what it was. I didn't want anything to do with that. I flat out ignored and moved on, paying extra attention to the questions asked during "diagnosing" appointments. It was my unique ability.

I think people struggle with this because they are working against themselves. They are trying to fit themselves in a predesigned box that does not serve them at ALL. The pain comes from trying to fit into a society that wasn't designed to accommodate or appreciate different abilities.

We have a choice. Let this limit you or let it set you free.

I caution you, my sweet friend, whatever labels you are carrying are a part of you not the whole of you. You are not damaged or flawed.

Your past does not define who you are. It was a lesson to teach you to be the person you needed to be to show up and serve the world with your unique abilities.

Though diagnosis can be an important piece of the puzzle, it is not the whole solution. Labels can give you direction, ways to manage the challenging parts of your life. They can help you find a community of others with a similar experience. These labels cannot be the whole story of you and why you are not showing up fully for your life. They cannot be your excuse, a crutch to stand upon to explain away why you can't live the life you want.

It's hard because we keep wishing it was different. We see it as the limitation to getting to our dreams. Stop imagining a life that you wish you would have had.

Stop looking for the instructions for a "normal" life. It doesn't exist. Stop trying to fit yourself into the image of what you think you are supposed to be in a world that was not designed for your unique abilities. Seek out others with your unique ability who are thriving and take note. How do they look at things? How do they handle the hard parts? How can you think of this differently? What if you didn't judge this as good or bad at all?

Labels have a way of wrapping assumptions on us. For as long as I remember, I identified as shy, so I played that part. It carried a shame for wanting to be braver and bolder and admiring others and how they show up with so much confidence. I truly believed that's who I was. I still am shy at times. I am still anxious and experience bouts of depression, but I don't live there anymore.

Maybe there's a reason ADHD labels are on the rise. This system isn't working and we are the early adaptors, the pioneers to the new world. Our unique way of thinking and abilities allow us to fill in gaps because we interpret the world in a very different way.

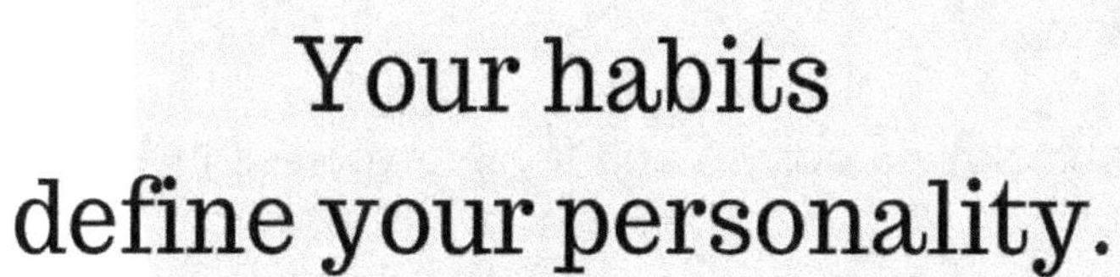

Your habits define your personality.

-Benjamin Hardy

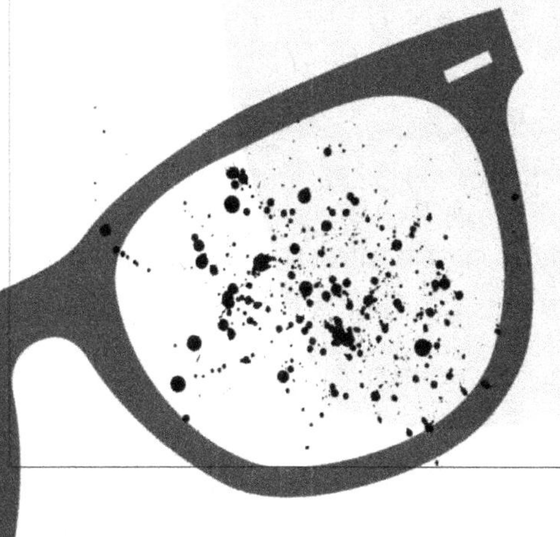

Workbook

What's a label you have been carrying? Do you like this label? Do you wish you could change it? How does it benefit you? How does it limit you?

What does the best version of you look like? What does that person act like?

Who do you admire and think to yourself I wish I could just be like them?

What is one itty-bitty action you could take to head in that direction?

For example:

I am shy. vs. I will practice being more outgoing and knowing what to say

Limitations: My ideas don't get shared. I don't contribute to the group. I have trouble making friends.

Benefits: observe others, great listener, low commitment, and follow-through.

Small actions to take to improve over time:

Use Mel Robins 5.4.3.2.1 - act on the impulse when it comes up to speak up in a group setting, even if it is suggesting where to eat. Repeat again and again until it's not hard. Join a special interest group, such as a Toastmasters group to be surrounded by others encouraging and supporting people, a safe place to share.

> *A favorite tip: Instead of a to-do list end your day with a TA-DA list. What are your 3 wins of the day? Write them down and congratulate yourself.*

Set up support:

Go with a friend. Tell a friend or loved one what you are working on. Journal progress - how did the first time feel, awful, never want to go back, go again anyway, less scary. See how your reactions and behaviors change over time. As a recovering social anxiety-stricken-shy person, this worked incredibly well for me.

Understand that most times you won't feel like it. It feels hard and it can still be scary but do it anyway and you will prove to yourself you can do hard things.

A note about decision making: there aren't any wrong decisions. As a recovering avoid-making-any-decision-and-pass-it-on-to-any-one-else type of person... I came to realize that any decision has ups and downs. If you end up making the "right" choice you gain or lose certain things, if you make the "wrong" decision you can equally loss or gain. At minimum you learn something from the experience which is always a win. It comes down to if you continue to give away your choices there is no shortage of people who will gladly take them, the down side is you may not like the choice they make and it can directly impact you and strip you of your power. Start small but start deciding for yourself the kind of person you want to show up as.

Chapter 22 – Ripple Effect

I woke up to the sounds of beeping around me, the room was dark, I felt groggy but I heard something. Sniffling? No, I knew that sound – soft, almost indistinguishable, enough to let the ache flow but stifled out of respect and pride.

I don't remember how I got here or much of what happened, I must have tried again. Dread creeped up as I realized another failed attempt, the 23rd. Another two weeks, more hospital time, endless questions, more pain to pass on to the family, as if I hadn't put them through enough. Why can't I just get this right already? I don't deserve to be alive. All I do is cause more problems for everyone.

I thought they were sleeping.

Pieces of the memory filter through. That sound again.

"Where is that coming from?" I think to myself.

Slowly, I start to push my eyes open. They feel heavy and sticky. I don't know how long I've been here. I hear movement.

I see a dark figure crouched down beside my bed. My eyes are blurry and without glasses it takes time to put the figure into focus. Dad? No. Doctor? No. Don!

Recognition hits me, I haven't seen Don for over a year. A wave of joy rises quickly then drops and is overtaken by shame. I am here again. Tears well up in my eyes, my chest hurts, my heart hurts because as I look down at Don, I feel the pang of guilt sitting on my chest.

He's there on a chair sitting by my bed. He holds my hand and hugs it to his collar.

"Hey," he says, "You're awake." He wipes his nose and runs a forearm across his brow.

I'm frozen in shock and shame. My words are caught in the desert of my throat.

He takes a deep breath, "It's ok, I brought you something".

He reaches into his jacket side and pulls out a little Christmas bear - white fur, dressed in red and green slacks, dulled gold buttons, and a matching hat affixed to the top of his head. Oh my gosh, its him.

Its Alex.

Don was a Child and Youth worker who was on the children's psychiatric ward. He was 6'2 burly guy. I remember when I met him, he reminded me of Frankenstein. Tall, strong frame and short cropped hair. I spent over 11 months in and out of hospital, living there for a month before I went to the larger facility. I spend a lot of time with the staff.

Don, Melissa and Stephanie where my favorites. We talked about real things, shared stories and they never judged me, I felt like they saw the real me, past the past the behavior, past the bullshit. They just saw me. They listened.

During my recovery time, Stacey and Melissa came to see me in the adult ward. They brought me a book. "Succulent Wild Women" by Sark. That book changed my life, but I don't think it would have been the same had Don not shared his corner of the triad.

Don always made us laugh, he was the best listener, and always saw the best in us. He was always up for a little fun and bending of the rules.

Once he even let us let us paint his finger nails pink and sparkly purple. He forgot to take it off and had training class the next day, approaching a distraught patient.

An instructor told him, "You look intimidating with your fists balled up like that. You need to open your hands up and relax, to inspire that feeling of calm in the patient. You look like you are ready to fight."

He had no choice, he showed off our incredible handy work. He was the laughing stock of the day.

He'd always share stories about a favorite childhood teddy bear. Alex was his name. Alex was quite the adventurous bear, getting into mischief and out of tight spots. Before he left at night, we'd ask him to say Hi to Alex for us. When we saw Don, he'd tell us what Alex had been up to. Alex played little tricks and left thoughtful surprise snacks on our side tables, funny notes and riddles. We never saw this mysterious Alex. Don was safe. He wasn't too old for play and make believe.

Now, there he was, eyes brimmed with tears, as he passed his beloved Alex to me.

I protested, stifled by the tubes and IVs, my body taking all its resources to heal the damage I had done, leaving little energy or moisture in my mouth to speak. Guilt and shame burning in my throat.

"It's ok, here." He lay Alex in my arms.

"Please don't" he said softly

"Please don't do this again. There is a whole life ahead of you. Alex is going to go with you now and keep you safe. You tell him your troubles. He's a great listener."

My eyes teared up. I didn't deserve his beloved childhood friend. His tears.

"Promise me" he said.

I looked down.

He lifted my chin. "Hey," He waited until my shifty eyes met his. "You'll figure this out, you are stronger than you know. You need to see you how the rest of us see you."

Still holding my hand, he put it up to his cheek. His cheek felt so warm on the back of my hand cold with the pump of IVs.

"Now you take care of Alex, he needs you now." He got up to go.

I had forgotten that moment until now.

Thinking back that was my last attempt.

I never saw Don again after that. After being kicked out I went to all the past places I knew to visit. I went back and to say thank you and hello and tell them I was doing alright. I learned Don was in security now. I learned his wife was having a baby soon. I came back a few days later with a gift and a note.

I told him that Alex was doing well and said "hi." I said that he came with me to find a new friend for Don and his baby. We picked the softest, sweetest bear and named him Mason. If he would, please take care of him now.

A few years later, I was at the hospital and I stopped in to see if I could find my friends from long ago. I wanted them to know I was doing so much better now. I didn't see them and for privacy and protection of the staff and patients, I couldn't learn more. A co-worker of Don's who remembered me told me he gave Don the gift. He said that Don and his wife had welcomed a baby boy and they named him Mason Alexander.

Have you ever watched rain drop into a pool of water? You see the rings expanding larger and larger. You see how wide they go and it's amazing that it came from one tiny drop. You are like that drop to the people around you. You impact them in unconscious ways all the time. They are taking in your example, your energy, they see things in you that you don't see in yourself. Often, they're the things you take for granted. Moods, energy, ideas – all contagious, for better or for worse. What part do you want to play?

What if we shifted our internal questions to what can I get excited about today? What is the lesson here to learn? What can I control? What do I get to do today? How can I help turn this around? How can I help another?

DON'T DO THE SAME THING FOR 75 YEARS AND CALL IT

A LIFE

ROBIN SHARMA

Chapter 23 – Final Thoughts: Embrace the Mess and Clean Your Glasses

It's been a busy day. I have had the privilege of having a day to paint. My husband has taken the boys. The itch to paint is real, I can taste it. I see the images dancing through my head. To feel the smooth contours of my brush, the paint I know will get all over my hands, a smatter on my clothes. It's a miracle any gets on the canvass, but somehow it does.

I have a question for you. Where is it you feel most at home? What is that place you go to that makes you smile just thinking about it.

Part of healing is finding a path back to doing the things that make you feel free. There are no expectations, no results, no timeline. It's a place for you to explore, tinker, and create. Is it telling stories, writing, painting, renovating, decorating, cooking, socializing, planning a trip?

I am often amazed how many people think they are not creative but their definition of creativity is limited. They think creativity is painting, drawing, sculpting, writing. Creativity, in its purest form, is playing with opposing ideas and finding a connection.

Art is not limited to art supplies but embodies craft in areas of life from cooking to sewing to laying out a solid argument for a case, to organizing a fantastic trip, or to finding a way to balance four kids' schedules, appointments, meal preferences, and allergies. It's the things that bring us joy.

I want you to take time to write down everything that brings you joy - things you've always wanted to do, that make you curious. Maybe it's a class, a conversation, a phone call. Maybe it's something you've always been fascinated with and haven't done. Is it an instrument you have always wanted to play? The point is to do it, a little bit. You don't have to commit huge. Find the joy in just showing up to see what happens and build it into your life a little at a time.

Your life is meant to be lived.

These moments tell stories and give your mind space to breathe and wonder, almost like an active meditative experience. Each experience holds an emotion, a feeling of a moment you can't remember until you see it there, while you are working. It's real and transformative, powerful and potent.

You may look at the fabric of your life so far and think what a mess. Compared to what? What do you think someone else's life must look like? Is it like the staged, neat versions we see on media?

Some might see a mess. I see a book of thoughts and stories that have made you the incredible person you are. Those experiences made you a strong and compassionate person who can see the pain in others and find a way to connect.

A bee wandered into my car the other day while we were driving, all the windows open. We tried to usher it outside unharmed (bees are endangered you know). This bee kept going in and out of the space where he was free and the danger of being in a car with frightened passengers trying to get him out. Even when we came to a full stop the bee continue to fly out then right back in wanting to go full speed at the windshield. He was already free and kept getting stuck trying to go where he could not.

You are already free. The windows are wide open and you can get out. You have been out for brief periods. It's what keeps you searching for the answers. The answers are never out there; they are within you.

Take pleasure knowing that this is YOUR glorious and beautiful mess. It is chaotic, scary, and so real.

This is the person you were not allowed to be out there in the real world. This is the one you learned to hide. This is the person who was just a little too weird, too wild, untamed. We learned to be small. We learned to cover ourselves in the layers that helped us be a part of our worlds.

I recently came across a book by Anne Lamont and the following words make me stop to hear them again and again - *"See*

I've always been a bit messy. I aim to live, albeit, in a bit of a rush, there are things I need to remember, things I have to do."

When I heard these words, I felt she had cracked the safe to my heart and let the door swing wide open. At that moment I had never felt so understood. She went on to say:

"Clutter and mess show us that life is being lived. Clutter is wonderfully fertile ground. You can still discover new treasures under all those piles, clean things up, edit things out, fix things, get a grip. Tidiness suggests that something is as good as it's going to get. Tidiness makes me think of held breath, of suspended animation, while life needs to breathe and move."

You are allowed to have a mess, loose ends, and feel angry and sad for what was, isn't, and what will never be. It's ok to let those memories and waves of emotion pass through. Don't stay there. Don't live in that space again and again. It happened. It's over. You came through.

You are here for more. There is work for you to do. What is it that whispers to your heart? What is that nagging little idea that keeps coming up? Who could you help? What impact could you make?

Show up as your most vibrant and beautiful self the way the smallest drop upon a pond great ripples forms, expanding wider and wider.

This is the gift of your experience. When it no longer traps you but feeds you, informs you, it gives you nutrients to grow.

Maybe it's gratitude and because of that gratitude, you find more joy to share.

"Life is supposed to be messy, alive, and full of possibility."

Let your mess feed imagination. Let it give rise to what could be, what has been lost what is calling to be found, reborn, reformed. When it's all perfect and complete, there is no room for wonder and reflection, no tickle of curiosity. It's all been thought out, all been considered.

Your glasses are going to get dirty from time to time. You'll lose your way and get off track. You can always pull them off, give them a wipe, and get out there and try again. I hope you do.

FIND HEALING IN THE THREADS OF YOUR STORY

ABOUT THE AUTHOR
LEAH SPELT L-I-G-I-A

Are you tired of saying no when you want to say yes? Are you tired of feeling afraid? She is no stranger to the trials and tribulations of that transition.

Leah takes you through her transformation— surpassing a childhood in chaos, a family wracked with mental health, all dying to have a new beginning, to living her dream and passion of art, creative storytelling, and enjoying her family.

She takes you through the journey to make sense of it all and gives you the tools and mindset it takes to show up empowered, brave, and as your vibrant self.

Leah spelt LIGIA fell in love with books and writing at an early age and never grew out of it.

When she is not correcting 1st time encounters with her name, she is working out for her next obstacle course with audiobooks pumping in her ears, painting in her studio, or hiking with her husband and kids.

Artist, writer, and public speaker, she loves sharing stories to entertain, inspire and uplift her audience to seek out the joyous parts of life. You can find her on YouTube.

Workshops and courses offered:

- **SAMH Survival Workshops**
- **Building confidence through effective communicati**
- **Isolation and burnout recovery**
- **-Clean your dirty glasses to thrive**
- **Personal Development**
- **Getting unstuck and into the flow**

To learn more visit: Leahspeltligia.com
For coaching and speaking inquiries:
E-mail: leahspeltligia@gmail.com
Connect on IG and FB: @leashspeltligia
Contact info: 226-388-4239
Visit my channel leahspeltligia on Youtube

To learn more and connect with Leah here:

Download your PDF workbook to start cleaning your dirty glasses:

SCAN HERE

Or visit: www.leahspeltligia.com

Follow on these platforms below

Or email leahspeltligia@gmail.com

About Defining Moments Press

Built for aspiring authors who are looking to share transformative ideas with others throughout the world, Defining Moments Press offers life coaches, healers, business professionals, and other non-fiction or self-help authors a comprehensive solution to getting their books published without breaking the bank or taking years.

Defining Moments Press prides itself on bringing readers and authors together to find tools and solutions.

As an alternative to self-publishing or signing with a major publishing house, we offer full profits to our authors, low-priced author copies, and simple contract terms.

Most authors get stuck trying to navigate the technical end of publishing. The comprehensive publishing services offered by Defining Moments Press mean that your book will be designed by an experienced graphic artist, available in printed, hard copy format, and coded for all eBook readers, including the Kindle, iPad, Nook, and more.

We handle all of the technical aspects of your book creation so you can spend more time focusing on your business that makes a difference for other people.

Defining Moments Press founder, publisher, and #1 bestselling author Melanie Warner has over 20 years of experience as a writer, publisher, master life coach, and accomplished entrepreneur.

You can learn more about Warner's innovative approach to self-publishing or take advantage of free trainings and education at: MyDefiningMoments.com.

Defining Moments Book Publishing

If you're like many authors, you have wanted to write a book for a long time, maybe you have even started a book...but somehow, as hard as you have tried to make your book a priority, other things keep getting in the way.

Some authors have fears about their ability to write or whether or not anyone will value what they write or buy their book. For others, the challenge is making the time to write their book or having accountability to finish it.

It's not just finding the time and confidence to write that is an obstacle. Most authors get overwhelmed with the logistics of finding an editor, finding a support team, hiring an experienced designer, and figuring out all the technicalities of writing, publishing, marketing, and launching a book. Others have actually written a book and might have even published it but did not find a way to make it profitable.

For more information on how to participate in our next Defining Moments Author Training program, visit: www.MyDefiningMoments.com. Or you can email melanie@MyDefiningMoments.com.

Other #1 Bestselling Books by Defining MomentsTM Press

Defining Moments: Coping With the Loss of a Child - Melanie Warner

Defining Moments SOS: Stories of Survival - Melanie Warner and Amber Torres

Write your Bestselling Book in 8 Weeks or Less and Make a Profit - Even if No One Has Ever Heard of You - Melanie Warner

Become Brilliant: Roadmap From Fear to Courage – Shiran Cohen

Unspoken: Body Language and Human Behavior For Business - Shiran Cohen

Rise, Fight, Love, Repeat: Ignite Your Morning Fire - Jeff Wickersham

Life Mapping: Decoding the Blueprint of Your Soul - Karen Loenser

Ravens and Rainbows: A Mother-Daughter Story of Grit, Courage and Love After Death – L. Grey and Vanessa Lynn

Pivot You! 6 Powerful Steps to Thriving During Uncertain Times – Suzanne R. Sibilla

A Workforce Inspired: Tools to Manage Negativity and Support a Toxic-Free Workplace – Dolores Neira

Journey of 1000 Miles: A Musher and His Huskies' Journey on the Century-Old Klondike Trails - Hank DeBruin and Tanya McCready

7 Unstoppable Starting Powers: Powerful Strategies For Unparalled Results From Your First Year as a New Leader – Olusegun Eleboda

Bouncing Back From Divorce With Vitality & Purpose: A Strategy For Dads – Nigel J Smart, PHD

Focus on Jesus and Not the Storm: God's Non-negotiables to Christians in America - Keith Kelley

Stepping Out, Moving Forward: Songs and Devotions - Jacqueline O'Neil Kelley

Time Out For Time In: How Reconnecting With Yourself Can Help You Bond With Your Child in a Busy Word - Jerry Le

The Sacred Art of Off Mat Yoga: Whisper of Wisdom Forever – Shakti Barnhill

The Beauty of Change: The Fun Way For Women to Turn Pain Into Power & Purpose – Jean Amor Ramoran

From No Time to Free Time: 6 Steps to Work/Life Balance For Business Owners - Christoph Nauer

Self-Healing For Sexual Abuse Survivors: Tired of Just Surviving, Time to Thrive - Nickie V. Smith

Prepared Bible Study Lessons: Weekly Plans For Church Leaders - John W. Warner

Frog on a Lily Pad - Michael Lehre

How to Effectively Supercharge Your Career as a CEO - Giorgio Pasqualin

Rising From Unsustainable: Replacing Automobiles and Rockets - J.P. Sweeney

Food - Life's Gift for Healing: Simple, Delicious & Life Saving Whole Food Plant Based Solutions - Angel and Terry Grier

Harmonize All of You With All: The Leap Ahead in Self-Development - Artie Vipperla

Powerless to Powerful: How to Stop Living in Fear and Start Living Your Life - Kat Spencer

Living with Dirty Glasses: Heal with Empathy - Leah Montani

The Road Back to You: Finding Your Way After Losing a Child to Suicide - Trish Simonson